D0287467

# MEN ARE FROM ISRAEL, WOMEN ARE FROM MOAB

## Insights About the Sexes from the Book of Ruth

DR. NORM WAKEFIELD
& JODY BROLSMA

InterVarsity Press
Downers Grove, Illinois

*InterVarsity Press*
*P.O. Box 1400, Downers Grove, IL 60515*
*World Wide Web: www.ivpress.com*
*E-mail: mail@ivpress.com*



*InterVarsity Press® is the book-publishing division of InterVarsity Christian Fellowship/USA®, a student movement active on campus at hundreds of universities, colleges and schools of nursing in the United States of America, and a member movement of the International Fellowship of Evangelical Students. For information about local and regional activities, write Public Relations Dept., InterVarsity Christian Fellowship/USA, 6400 Schroeder Rd., P.O. Box 7895, Madison, WI 53707-7895.*



*ISBN 0-8308-2258-5*

*Printed in the United States of America ∞*

---

**Library of Congress Cataloging-in-Publication Data**

*Wakefield, Norm.*
*Men are from Israel, women are from Moab: insights about the sexes from the book of Ruth/Norm Wakefield & Jody Brolsma.*
*p. cm.*
*Includes bibliographical references (p.).*
*ISBN 0-8308-2258-5 (paper: alk. paper)*
*1. Man-woman relationships—Religious aspects—Christianity. 2. Communication in marriage. 3. O.T. Ruth—Criticism, interpretation, etc. I. Brolsma, Jody. II. Title.*
*BT705.8.W34 2000*
*261.8'357—dc21*

*00-039584*

---

*16 15 14 13 12 11 10 9 8 7 6 5 4*
*12 11 10 09 08 07 06 05 04*

*To Erik . . . my Boaz.*

—JODY BROLSMA

*This book is dedicated to the hardworking women*
*I've had the joy of working with*
*over the past several years*
*at Phoenix Seminary.*
*They have consistently exhibited*
*the spirit of Ruth:*
*Kristin Beasley, Kay Dubois, Steffanie Johnson,*
*Roma Royer, Kristin Smith, Sharon Sullivan,*
*Kathy Thompson and Janelle Wood.*

—DR. NORM WAKEFIELD

# Contents

# 1

# The Problem

THE IDEA FOR THIS BOOK HAS BEEN STEWING IN MY BRAIN FOR several years. But the roots of it go back even further. Listen as I share some of those thoughts with you.

"When I get married my wife and I will never argue." This was my rock solid resolution more than thirty-five years ago, and I meant it! I'd felt enough anxiety and pain of family hostility in my childhood to last a lifetime. And beyond this circle I'd observed plenty of husbands and wives "picking" at each other, belittling each other and competing with each other. When I stood at the altar ready to cross that threshold, I wanted peace in my home.

To be honest, my rock-solid resolution didn't last very long. Like most couples, Winnie and I branded each other with our red-hot arguments.

While my marriage has been my most intimate and intense relationship, my life has been spent investing in relationships. I've not manufactured many "widgets," but I've sure connected with a lot of people. Winnie and I have reared five children and now have five grandchildren. Vocationally I've lived a pastoral lifestyle. Almost every day I'm interacting with people as a friend, teacher, mentor or counselor. I've invested thousands of hours helping individuals unlearn destructive and unfulfilling relational attitudes and habits and teaching them how to replace them with positive attitudes and skills.

These experiences have left me a wealthy man—in terms of friendships and precious memories. I've tasted the sweetness of invigorating relationships. I've bonded with individuals who encouraged my heart, stimulated my thinking and left their fingerprints on my life. I've also encountered individuals who were bossy, controlling and demanding. I've retreated from individuals who were intimidating, hostile and argumentative. And I've empathized with individuals who were fearful, insecure and lonely.

While there are many interpersonal challenges, one overriding observation has pursued me like a hound tracking a fox. I've become more and more troubled by the relational barrier that exists between men and women. I consistently read of it in books, periodicals and the newspaper. "The war between the sexes" sells well.

We live in a society that is frantically trying to define how men and women should live and interact together. We work together, study together and play together. Yet the more we pursue mutuality, the more relationships between men and women become elusive, fragile and tense. Hostility keeps rearing its ugly head like a menacing cobra. Sexual harassment is a hot button. What we are trying to find eludes us. In fact, warring between the sexes seems to be more intense, more aggressive and more hostile than ever.

This saddens but does not surprise me. Sin undermines, distorts and corrupts relationships. I can comprehend that men and women who do not know of the love of Christ can become alienated from each other and establish relational barriers. This troubles me, and it's painful to see such a pervasive violation of relationships.

But I feel a deeper ache. I observe alienation within Christ's family, the body of Christ. Attitudes and behaviors that wound and distance men and women are too often present here. So I ask myself, *Why do we who have experienced Christ's redeeming love not lavish that on each other as men and women? What evil poisons our relationships and keeps us acting in such destructive ways?*

Recently my daughter Amy, son-in-law Mike and grandson Tony were traveling from Loveland, Colorado, to our home in Phoenix, Arizona. Because long trips often create boredom, someone suggested an "imagine that" game. *"Imagine that you could go back to any time in the past. Where would you go?"*

Mike said, "I'd like to go back to the Garden of Eden."

That's a creative idea! What would Mike hope to discover in Eden? What impression do we have of that original garden? What makes it such an appealing place? What would it be like to spend a day there? What would we "ooh" and "aah" about when we returned?

If I could have been that unobserved visitor in the garden, I would have watched how Adam and Eve treated each other without sin's damning interference. How did they relate? How did they speak to each other? How did they work together? Did they argue over who would do what? Did one have to be in control? Did they laugh together with joy and spontaneity? Was there freedom and transparency between them?

My bet is we'd envy what we saw. We'd notice right away that they had an indescribable relational freedom. I'll bet they laughed together, played together and worked together with an innocence and zest that would leave us feeling envious. We'd be saying, "I wish my relationships were like that."

But an evil monster subtly slipped into the Garden. Sin injected its evil poison, contaminating this pure, joyful relationship. And life has never been the same since. Our foreparents would never again have that spontaneous freedom, that innocent joy. Life would never again be so much fun. And we too have been infected.

### The Roots of Relational Tension

Yes, on that fateful day Adam and Eve's lives were traumatically changed. Forever. The freedom, joy and fulfillment they'd known simply vanished. Through the enticement of the serpent Eve made a fatal decision that forever distorted everything she'd known. Shortly thereafter Adam partnered in the sin, and he too was infected with its venom.

Make no mistake, *sin* created a tension between men and women. The barrier it created can be traced throughout the course of human history.

The sin had an immediate effect on Adam and Eve's relationship. When the Lord faced them with their sin, Adam's response was, "The woman you put here with me—she gave me some fruit from the tree, and I ate it" (Genesis 3:12). Adam distanced himself from Eve, attempting to credit her with evil motives. Blame became a new human strategy to cope with sin. Perhaps Adam thought, *If it wasn't for her, I wouldn't be in this mess. I'm going to have to start looking out for number one.*

When the Lord defined the consequences of sin on their

lives, he identified this new relational distance. The Lord said, "Your desire will be for your husband, and he will rule over you" (Genesis 3:16). Thus sin introduced a new hierarchy of relationship that exists to this day. Men and women have struggled with "one upmanship" since the Fall.

Don't miss this point. Sin skewed the creative balance between man and woman. Sin created a tension in relationships that has resulted in pain, discouragement and alienation ever since. I don't mean to say that in a given situation a man and woman cannot live in peace and treat each other with dignity and respect. Obviously that has happened many times. But the larger historical picture bears out the tragic destructive tension that has existed between men and women.

As I read through the Scriptures, I watch for clues to this underlying tension between man and woman. I see it in Sarai, Hagar and Abram as they manipulate each other to "help" the Lord produce offspring for them (Genesis 16:1-5). It infiltrates the relationship between Rebekah and Isaac, leaving it tainted with suspicion, mistrust and manipulation (Genesis 27). And then there's Samson and Delilah—a pathetic example of a man and woman manipulating each other for personal gain. Even Hosea and Gomer are forced to live with mistrust and hurt.

And each incident leaves a painful wound, simmering resentment and a sense of emptiness—tragic results.

Let's be honest. Sin poisons our relationships. Most of us exhibit its effect. Only when we admit we're sick do we have the potential to get well.

**Creative Tension Today**

By the time this book is in print I will be sixty-five years old. In my earliest memories I felt the subtle alienation between men and women. The older I've grown, the more obvious—and more painful—it's become. Such alienation displays itself in many forms; it has several characteristics. I want to underscore that these are not true of every relationship between a man and woman. But they are general patterns that tend to characterize gender relationships.

First, the majority of men and women don't enjoy talking with each other on a transparent, vulnerable level. When they do speak to each other, it's often superficial or "small talk." In fact, in most social gatherings you'll observe men and women in separate groups. Men huddle with "the guys" talking about "guy things" while women are clustered together, chatting about "women things." Of course, I recognize that there are exceptions to what I'm describing, but they are just that—exceptions. Society explains this phenomena by saying, "Men and women are different, so it's just a natural thing." I don't agree. I believe it is one of the consequences of the sin that originated in the Garden of Eden.

Second, men and women tend to develop their own gender vocabulary that creates a "gender" club. Men have developed their set of rules and initiation rites that exclude women. Women do the same. These deeply rooted patterns get passed on to new generations, with the perennial results of alienated relationships. It's easy to see it in the other sex, but too often we are reluctant to admit that we are as much a part of the problem as they are.

In our generation a sophisticated belief developed that men and women are irreparably different, and the best way to exist is to admit the difference and learn to live with it. "Men are rational; women are emotional" is a convenient catchphrase to get us off the hook. We smile, nod our heads in agreement as though we've solved the problem, and go on with our gender-soaked conversation.

By stressing how different we are, we've invented a convenient excuse to avoid facing what sin has done to us. (We'll explore the issue of differences later, but for now we merely want you to recognize the greater problem it creates—continued alienation.)

My third observation is that the tension and alienation between men and women leads to a fundamental disrespect for each other. Too often men and women exist in a shallow relationship but never genuinely *enjoy* the relationship or allow it to become rich and fruitful. Without respect men and women learn to demean each other, causing hurt and deeper separation. Tragically we've become comfortable living with an empty, unfulfilling relationship.

We try to pass laws that will guarantee interpersonal rights. The problem is that laws never deal with the root cause. If anything, they often create a deeper alienation. Laws will never resolve the problem because laws don't change an individual's heart. Often they only widen the gap, because we invent clever and creative ways to continue our alienation. And everyone loses.

**Creative Tension in the Church**

I can understand how a society alienated from Jesus Christ becomes entrenched in tension and alienation between men and women. But it's disturbing to see the same pattern existing within the church—Christ's body! We boast that we're redeemed people. We say that we are following the God of love. If this is so, why doesn't this impact our relationships in a significant way?

Let me describe a few scenarios that visualize my concern.

**Scenario 1**

I attended a church several years ago that had strong male leadership. Men taught all adults. I noted godly, gifted women who were eager to utilize their spiritual gifts. They wanted to explore opportunities for teaching ministry among the women of the church. They were not pushy or demanding. The leaders reaction could best be described as "You are dear sweet women. Just sit still, be quiet and watch." I cringed as I watched the vision and energy of gifted and talented women wither and die. What a tragic loss!

(Recently a friend attended a church that had two kinds of membership—voting and nonvoting. The men could vote, the women couldn't!)

**Scenario 2**

At a church retreat individuals were randomly paired up to go on an "Emmaus walk." During the first fifteen minutes one person would share while the other listened. Then the second person would share for fifteen minutes, and person number one would listen. After that event a friend of mine reported on his walk with a woman, "For the first time in my life I really listened to a woman. I'm ashamed to admit that I've always felt that women had nothing of importance to say. So I've never listened." (This man had been married for over twenty years. Imagine what his wife had been feeling!)

**Scenario 3**

Sam has a sincere love for Jesus Christ. He also is a devoted husband and father. He relates to his children in a warm and compassionate manner. When dealing with behavioral problems, he is thoughtful and intuitive in his response. Yet his wife belittles him because he isn't tough and logical in dealing with discipline. "Why can't you be like other men?" she laments.

**Our Intent**

Jody and I want to challenge you to think along as we grapple with the issue we've raised. Although this book is the result of the efforts of both authors, for the sake of clarity you'll find that the "I" refers to Norm throughout the book. I value my writing partner, who also happens to be my daughter. She is a gifted writer, one who loves Jesus Christ and a woman who is committed to the biblical truths we describe in this book. I believe that our own relationship embodies these precious truths. Our prayer is that your heart will be open to consider our loving Father's challenge to us as men and women.

# 2

# A Biblical Model of Gender

JOHN GRAY'S WILDLY POPULAR BOOK *MEN ARE FROM MARS, Women Are from Venus* seems to have struck a chord in many people's minds and emotions. It remained on the *New York Times Review of Books* bestseller list for over two hundred weeks. The assumption underlying the book is that men and women are radically different—so different that their spaceships arrived from different planets.

Perhaps one reason Gray's book is so appealing is that it scratches people where they itch. It seems to explain the nagging irritation they feel.

"Where did he get that idea?"

"Honestly! I don't understand her at all!"

Men and women attempt to relate to each other and frequently fail miserably. Often it seems that they are unable to communicate at all. To some the hope of a satisfying relationship is like a sick joke. The chasm in many male-female relationships is as wide and deep as the Grand Canyon and leads to a hopeless despair. There's no Golden Gate Bridge long enough to span this chasm. Thus, the suggestion that we are radically different in our makeup makes people feel better when their attempts at relating collapse.

Parallel to this struggle is contemporary research in gender differences. We poke, prod, x-ray, analyze and codify in the name of scientific research to "prove" how different we are. I do not mean to attack or demean valid research. It's obvious that there are plenty of fundamental differences between men and women. But there is danger in *overemphasizing* our differences and losing sight of powerful, enriching elements that we share in common.

**What Color Are Your Sunglasses?**

Paradigms are fascinating critters. A paradigm is a grid through which we view life. It's like a pair of internal sunglasses. Once sunglasses are on, we forget that they are changing the "color" of the world we are viewing. Have you ever stepped inside on a sunny day still wearing your sunglasses? Or driven into a darkened parking garage with your sunglasses still on? What happens? You're temporarily blinded until you take them off. We assume that the environment we are seeing is being viewed as it really is. The sunglasses have helpfully distorted the true color and light. Sunglasses are valuable as long as we acknowledge that they have filtered out some of our world.

In the same way, paradigms filter our world. They help us set boundaries and make sense of life. They allow us to live comfortably so we don't have to reexamine something every time we encounter it. When you pick up a deck of cards, you always know which is a king, queen or jack because it is always the same figure. It would be frustrating if we had to learn new symbols every time we wanted to play a game of cards.

We all use paradigms to make sense of our world. In fact, it would be difficult to live without them. But as with sunglasses, we sometimes forget that we are looking at life through our paradigms. We fail to remember that we are filtering our incoming data and experience. And over time we begin to assume that everything we believe is true to life.

Examining or changing paradigms is not always easy. Many of us feel uncomfortable because something that seemed secure is taken away or altered. But it can be costly when my paradigm is robbing me of an opportunity to experience a richer, more fulfilling life. It's a great loss when I need to change my paradigm, and I'm unwilling to do it.

For many years the Swiss were known as the master watchmakers. Up until the mid-1960s they controlled about 85 percent of the market. Then someone invented the quartz movement and incorporated it into watches. When Swiss watchmakers saw it at a tradeshow, they chuckled. "What an odd looking gadget! Who would buy a watch that didn't have hands and springs?" They couldn't grasp that a new paradigm was just around the corner. (They'd forgotten to remove their sunglasses!)

But individuals at Texas Instruments and Seiko weren't laughing. They envisioned a radically new concept in watches. So they purchased the rights to manufacture quartz crystal watches, and within ten years the Swiss had only 10 percent of the market. As many as fifty thousand Swiss watchmakers became unemployed. The paradigm switch cost them dearly.

**Our Cultural Sunglasses**

It seems to us that "enlightened" people today have become

trapped in a cultural paradigm that shapes how they see themselves as men and women. Our society keeps focusing on gender differences and fails to recognize the importance of what is shared in common. This is doubly important to those who profess to follow Jesus Christ. The Word of God says that "if anyone is in Christ, he is a new creation; the old has gone, the new has come" (2 Corinthians 5:17). Now there's a paradigm switch!

Our Lord has introduced us to this new paradigm of reality. It's rooted in how he sees life—our Lord's reality. Speaking through the prophet Isaiah, God says, "My thoughts are not your thoughts, neither are your ways my ways. . . . As the heavens are higher than the earth, so are my ways higher than your ways, and my thoughts than your thoughts" (Isaiah 55:8-9).

Seeing truth in a new light—from our Lord's perspective—can transform our lives. And it can transform our relationships as men and women. We err when we try to squeeze our Lord into our world—to make him fit our paradigm. It's true that when Jesus Christ came in human flesh, he entered the world of humanity. And this may lead us to think that he should adapt himself to our point of view. But Jesus' aim is to draw us into his world. He is asking us to admit that he has the ultimate view of reality. God asks us to let him bring us into his reality. And that changes everything.

What our Lord is pursuing is no small task. We are so accustomed to seeing things our way that it is difficult to visualize something that we have never considered before. At the time of this writing I am trying to learn Spanish on my own. I have a dear friend, Lalo Vargas, who is Bolivian but lives in the United States. Lalo is helping me begin to think like a Bolivian. He's teaching me how a Bolivian would speak Spanish. That requires me to accept new ways of thinking that seem strange to me—a new paradigm. What Lalo says doesn't make sense to the way I've been taught to think, but it's essential that I trust my friend if I'm ever to learn Spanish.

**Laying a Solid Foundation**

We'd like to challenge your paradigm with some preliminary thoughts. You may or may not feel comfortable with them. But try them on for size, because they provide foundational concepts for our pursuit.

Christian men and women are more alike than they are different. How we see each other is the basis for how we relate to each other. If we see each other as enormously different, then we will think there is little common ground for our relationship. And our behavior will follow the belief. But if we are convinced that we share many things in common, we'll want to find out what they are and let them become the footing for a healthy, growing relationship.

Let's return to my adventure in Spanish. Because I am learning this as I continue other activities, the progress seems agonizingly slow. A few weeks ago I was at the Mayo Clinic in Scottsdale, Arizona, in the ophthalmology department. Seated across from me were a husband and wife from Mexico. I knew that they were Christians, but neither of us knew the other person's language. Yet because of our bonds in Christ we both wanted to communicate. A precious reality linked our lives. So although the interchange was comical at times, it was also fun because we knew there were things we wanted to say to each other. I came away from the clinic joyful in spirit because two men's lives had touched in spite of their language barriers.

An observer might have said, "You two are so different that there is no basis for a relationship. You're kidding yourselves. It's hopeless!" But from our Lord's perspective the two men shared too much in common to forego an interaction. We *had* to try to communicate. If I were to meet my new friend Melesio Gurrola again, we would smile and take up where we left off.

It makes a world of difference whether we focus on how different we are or how much we share in common. It's like the parent who focuses on her child's weaknesses rather than his strengths. The weaknesses consume all her attention. They are the center of her concern. They exhaust her energy. And they shape the relationship. But the parent who builds on the child's strengths will find them shaping the relationship and nurturing a more positive, healthy interaction.

Have you noticed that wherever people's differences are emphasized, it leads to alienation and conflict? (Think of the racial tensions of the 1960s.) The problem with most of today's men-women focus is that it magnifies gender differences, which widens the gap and too often leads to conflict. The commitment to find common ground isn't there.

### A Biblical Model for Men and Women

Have you ever noticed that when you read through the Bible, you don't find many examples of positive relationships between men and women? That's not because our Lord didn't intend it to be that way. Rather, it's a clear testimony to the pervasive effect of sin on human relationships. Probably the most telling evidence of sin's destructive effect on Adam and Eve's relationship is its continued power to alienate men and women. But there is hope.

There is one Old Testament book that contains a profound example of a healthy, positive relationship between a man and two women. It is the book of Ruth. This fascinating account opens with a Jewish husband and wife, Elimelech and Naomi, trying to cope with famine in Israel. They choose to escape these conditions by relocating in the pagan land of Moab.

There they rear their two sons, Mahlon and Chilion, who intermarry with Moabite women (a practice violating God's law). Then Elimelech and his two sons die, leaving Naomi destitute with two daughters-in-law. She determines to return to her homeland, where conditions have improved, and she urges Orpah and Ruth to remain in Moab.

In a tearful departure Orpah decides to remain in Moab, but with a determined conviction Ruth forsakes her homeland and travels to Israel with her mother-in-law. They arrive in the village of Bethlehem destitute of family or income. Ruth decides to go into the fields that are being harvested and gather the grain that the harvesters have overlooked.

In a fateful event she enters the field of a prosperous landowner, Boaz. In these remarkable circumstances these two individuals—a poor but godly woman and a wealthy but godly man—are able to look beyond significant outward differences. Instead they see into each other's heart and discover there godly qualities of a humble and loving person. The relationship that emerges changes their lives forever.

I have read and reread that account countless times and continue to be intrigued by what it teaches. Without question it is a powerful testimony of what the love of our Lord can do in the lives of a man and a woman.

It is our conviction that the Lord allowed this small book to be recorded as a witness to us all, pointing us to what he desires in our relationships. This book you hold in your hands explores the dynamics of this lovely, godly relationship between Ruth and Boaz. We believe that Ruth and Boaz are a biblical model of transformation applied to gender relationships. Through them our Lord gives us a picture-window view of his vision for men and women.

A word of caution. Many people can't resist the urge to frame

Ruth and Boaz's relationship in a modern context—or should we say *paradigm*—where relationships like this are based on romantic attraction. They credit this remarkable relationship to an emotional infatuation. They want to see romantic sparks fly between the two. The text does not support this teaching. We're merely trying to read something in that we want to be there. A careful study of the text reveals that their remarkable relationship was rooted in solid spiritual convictions. The fact that the account ends in marriage is a testimony to their character, not their hormones.

In introducing this study we believe it is necessary to suggest some overarching principles. They help us begin to see our Lord's view for relationships.

The key to positive, healthy relationships between Christian men and women is godly character. Biblical character qualities are the basis for all relationships but are of strategic importance between men and women. To begin with, consider the fruit of the Spirit identified in Galatians 5:22-23: "But the fruit of the Spirit is love, joy, peace, patience, kindness, goodness, faithfulness, gentleness and self-control. Against such things there is no law."

The fruit of the Spirit is not something that can be imposed on an individual. We cannot establish laws to make people loving, joyful, kind or gentle. These qualities come from the inside out. Though we are tempted to pressure people to conform to a standard of conduct, our Lord's plan is to transform the inner person so the result is twenty times more powerful—it's life changing. Colossians 3:12-17 also describes this inner process of transformation through our relationship with Christ that results in a transformation of all of our relationships.

Men and women in Christ share the gifts of the Spirit without regard to gender (1 Corinthians 12:1-27). Men and women need each other to become mature, healthy individuals in Christ. And we will never become a mature, healthy family of God apart from freely giving and receiving what our Lord has placed in each of us. We need each other as men and women, expressing some unique aspect of our Lord's life. We cannot afford to be divided or prejudiced toward each other. Otherwise everyone loses.

Notice that 1 Corinthians 12 describes positive differences that attract us to each other. We say, "I admire what our Lord has invested of himself in you that is lacking in me. It invigorates me and stimulates growth in my life." His way is different from our human tendency. We focus on what we perceive as negative differences and allow them to alienate us from each other. He draws us to positive differences that he has purposely planted within us, so we learn to esteem one another and admit that we need each other.

Men are touched by specific character qualities in women; women are impacted by specific character qualities in men. Our Lord has no double standard for men and women. All inner qualities are to be pursued by both men and women. These qualities are to be lived out among Christians without regard to gender, race, culture, position or age. Our Lord really means it when he calls us to the fellowship of all believers—not the fellowship of men and the fellowship of women. To deny our unity and sense of corporateness (that transcends gender) violates one of the most important aspects of what it means to be a child of God.

Having stated the above, *we believe that men are attracted to certain character qualities in women, and women are attracted to certain character qualities in men.* Let me give two examples (expanded upon in later chapters).

Healthy women are attracted to gentle men. Ironically our

society more often identifies gentleness as a feminine trait. Yet the Bible holds up men as the model of gentleness (Matthew 11:29; 1 Thessalonians 2:7; 1 Timothy 3:3; 2 Timothy 2:25). What we are saying here is that both men and women should pursue gentleness, but it is especially attractive in a man because our society does not place a high value on gentleness in men—but God does.

Healthy men are attracted to strong women. By strong women we mean much more than physical strength. Healthy men find a woman of emotional and spiritual strength attractive because healthy men do not want women to be weak. They admire women who have vision. They enjoy seeing women use their talents, gifts and strength to achieve worthy goals. Only sick men try to keep women weak and under their control.

As we investigate the relationship between Ruth and Boaz, we will find specific inner qualities that attracted Ruth to Boaz. They are still qualities that women admire in men. In like manner we will find specific qualities that attract Boaz to Ruth. When we use the word *attract,* we are not speaking of romantic attraction. We identify them as character attractiveness. It is the beauty of the inner life, not physical features, power or position.

**Healthy Men and Women?**

You probably noticed the use of the phrases "healthy women are . . ." and "healthy men are . . ." in the previous paragraphs. Frankly not all of us are emotionally and spiritually healthy. We may be carriers of relational "diseases" and either not know it or not know what to do about it. An emotionally and spiritually healthy person exhibits the following characteristics:

- ☐ has the ability to accept and embody our Lord's stated reality
- ☐ has the ability to give as well as receive
- ☐ has the ability to adapt to needed change

☐ lives out the compassionate love of Christ in all relationships
☐ is honest about personal prejudices and negative actions that undermine positive relationship
☐ relates to others in a mutually satisfying manner

Although we are the authors of this book, we share with you the challenge of the statements listed above. We are committed to them, and this forces us to be open to our Lord's sovereign leadership in our lives. We too have felt the challenge to "grow up" in new ways, and we expect this to continue until we are called "home." We ask you to join us in growing up in Christ.

**The Challenge Before Us**

One of the primary ways our Lord stimulates growth in us is by allowing us to face circumstances that urge us beyond the status quo and motivate us to let Christ's beauty be formed in us. The New Testament writer James reminds us that we should "consider it pure joy . . . whenever you face trials of many kinds, because you know that the testing of your faith develops perseverance. Perseverance must finish its work so that you may be mature and complete, not lacking anything" (James 1:2-4). We know our Lord loves us beyond description, but sometimes we fail to see that his love challenges us to move to new levels of maturity.

Some of our most significant growth occurs as we face formidable hurdles, but genuine, life-changing growth is ours if we have the courage to open ourselves to it. At times we may feel uncomfortable because it may challenge our old paradigm. We may find ourselves challenged to change our past relational habits. These changes may feel awkward, embarrassing or humbling at first. But our Lord promises that his Spirit will empower us as we seek to be men and women who incarnate his beauty (Ephesians 1:19, 3:16-20; Colossians 1:11).

**What's Here for Us?**

We want you to interact with the ideas in this book. Therefore, we will raise questions that will challenge your thinking and suggest a course of action. As you prepare to face Ruth and Boaz consider these questions:

1. Who has shaped how I think and feel about persons of the opposite sex?

2. How do I typically deal with new and uncomfortable situations? New ideas? Am I willing to be made uncomfortable by seeing where I need to grow relationally? If not, why?

3. What tangible evidence can I give that indicates that I want to live in unity of spirit with members of the opposite sex?

4. What common ground has our Lord given men and women?

# 3

# A Man of Grace

MARTIN WAS THE BRIGHTEST STAR IN THE PITCH-BLACK SKY. His devotion to Jesus Christ was an inspiration to earnest truth seekers. Others looked to him for leadership, and his zeal and commitment to the Word of God was obvious. But there was a downside. Martin was not always easy to live with.

One day his friend Philipp received a letter from John, another Christian leader. John described Martin with the following words:

> [He] allows himself to be carried beyond all bounds with his love of thunder. We all of us acknowledge that we are much indebted to him. But in the Church we must always be upon our guard, lest we pay too great a deference to men. It is all over when a single individual has more authority than all the rest. Where there is so much division and separation as we now see, it is indeed no

> easy matter to still the troubled waters and bring about composure. You will say that [Martin] has a vehement disposition and ungovernable impetuosity. Let us, therefore, bewail the calamity of the Church and not devour our grief in silence. While you dread to meddle with this question, you are leaving in perplexity and suspense very many persons who require from you somewhat a more certain sound on which they can repose.[1]

John Calvin penned this letter to Philipp Melanchthon, a close associate of the firebrand reformer Martin Luther. It seems that Martin was not always gracious toward others.

Charles T. Studd was an early missionary pioneer to Africa. He too exhibited a burning love for Jesus Christ. He gave away a financial fortune and turned his eyes toward untouched mission fields. His passion to reach the lost drove him like a raging wildfire. He labored long, fatiguing hours and made immense personal sacrifices. But he also placed unrealistic expectations on others, requiring them to match his energy level—and when they couldn't live up to it, he became critical and judgmental. Relationships were impaired or destroyed. He even neglected his ailing and lonely wife.[2]

---

*"Greatness lies not in being strong,*
*but in the right use of strength."*
***Henry Ward Beecher***

---

Martin and Charles left their indelible mark on Christian history. But they also left behind damaged relationships. Though they embraced and defended the grace of God, they were not always effective in modeling it.

Other men and women who live in relative obscurity touch individuals' lives deeply with warmth and grace. Think of the aged woman who stood before a young man and cupped his cheeks in her weathered hands. As their eyes met, he felt the devotion they expressed. A year before he had arrived at the Navajo reservation as an inquiring outsider. His doctoral studies had brought him to investigate these people and their culture. He ate, slept and worked among them, sharing their lifestyle as fully as possible, to more fully understand their ways

An unusual friendship developed. In a remarkable way the young student and the ancient woman formed a loving bond that transcended language. He learned snippets of Navajo, she bits and pieces of English. Yet their heart-to-heart communication was rich, deep and powerful.

The day of his departure had arrived. His hand reached to open the vehicle door. With tears streaming down her cheeks she spoke. "*I like me best when I'm with you.*" The words she uttered etched themselves on his heart forever. Whenever he thought of them, his heart was warmed.

Almost two thousand years earlier another woman's heart was also etched with love. She experienced life-changing grace in an encounter with an unforgettable person. She came trudging down a dusty road on that hot day to fill her water pot. Her thirsting heart matched her thirsting lips. At the well she met a man who had paused there to rest.

After a few sentences of conversation with him she knew that she'd met a man who was different from all the other men she'd known. Their meeting probably lasted less than an hour. But she, like the elderly woman, hurried away to tell her friends about one who filled her life with joy and hope. She had met Jesus Christ.

**The Secret Ingredient**

What is this critical element that distinguished the men we've looked at? What is this ingredient that determines whether relationships are positive or negative—the ingredient that is critical to relationships' success, health and prosperity? What is the element that leads individuals to lasting commitment? Is there a special "something" that makes the difference? If so, what is it?

It is grace.

*Grace is the defining attraction in any significant, meaningful relationship. Grace is the bonding agent that allows vibrant life to flow from one individual to another. Grace* is the New Testament word that defines our relationship with our Lord. The apostle Paul said that we "stand" in this grace (Romans 5:2). Our Lord's heart of grace opened the treasure vaults of heaven and invited us to receive all of heaven's blessings that flow from this bottomless source of love (Ephesians 1:3).

---

*"The word 'grace' is unquestionably the most significant single word in the Bible."*
**Ilion T. Jones**

---

For years I have been motivated to investigate, ponder, grapple with and taste this grace relationship our Lord extends to us. The longer I've studied it in the Bible and experienced it in my life, the more I've realized that I was called to incarnate grace in my relationships with others. It became obvious that it is *the* critical element to any profound, loving human relationship. Without grace the relationship is never infused with the energy to nurture another life.

We mistakenly believe that if we gather enough truth about our Lord, our spouse, our children, our friends, and so on, we will be successful in relating to them. What we fail to realize is that *grace, not truth,* is that miraculous adhesive that bonds us to each other. (Both grace and truth are inseparable essential elements in living the Christian life. Our Lord never intends them to be separated—see John 1:14. What I'm saying here is that one unique function of grace is to bind us together relationally.)

---

*"When God measures a person, he puts the tape around the heart, not around the head."*
***Anonymous***

---

In the early years of my marriage I would sometimes correct my wife, Winnie, saying, "Anyone who has read on this subject knows . . ." I was trying to "straighten her out" with truth! I discovered that Winnie didn't appreciate having truth thrown in her face. Later I found that grace is much more powerful and compassionate.

One reason we place high value on grace in our relationships is because grace plows the soil of the heart and makes it receptive to receive the seeds that we may want to drop into the soil. Grace cultivates the soil so that when truth is spoken, the person is open and receptive. When the spirit of grace is my *lifestyle* toward others, I speak to them, and they are more apt to accept and profit from what I say. Seeds of truth need to fall in grace-saturated soil.

Our tendency is to separate grace and truth, and act as though we can embrace one without the other. (You're probably stronger or more comfortable with one than the other, right?) Jesus Christ never did that; he was "full of grace and truth" (John 1:14). He challenges us to allow both elements to permeate our lives so that we can become whole and healthy individuals. Grace and truth go together, but in the early stages of a relationship grace needs to lead the way to make the heart ready for truth. This allows truth to have its fullest jolt. *What we're stressing here is that we are better at telling others what they can or can't do rather than creating a healthy relational environment in which truth can be incarnated.* That's why others don't respond as we think they should.

**Boaz: A Gracious Man**

Boaz is one of a select few Old Testament models of grace. He lived grace. He led by grace. He spoke grace. He radiated grace.

We see quickly that his actions are positive, caring actions that draw others to his loving concern for them. Like the Samaritan woman at the well looking at Jesus, they say, "This man is unusual. He's different from other men I've met. I find him appealing."

Both men and women can be filled with God's grace, but it is especially powerful to see it in a man. Women are attracted to gracious men who don't rely on a "macho" image for their identity, but on this more powerful inner attribute. What is fascinating about grace is that it doesn't rest on attitudes or actions that are meant to emphasize "Look who I am!" but on attitudes and actions that say, "How can I serve or bless you? What can I give you?" This is a radiant attractiveness!

---

*"Kindness has converted more sinners than zeal, eloquence or learning."*
***Fredrick Faber***

---

**Grace Penetrates the Heart**

Boaz was a prosperous farmer. But many people in that culture lived from day to day depending on men like Boaz to provide work. There was no health insurance, no social security, no worker's compensation. It was a challenge to have the basic necessities of life.

So Boaz enters the field among workers who are dependent

on him for their daily needs. But standing in the wings are those like Ruth who aren't even employees. She's an Old Testament "street person" hoping to pick up the scant leftovers others have overlooked.

Boaz is surrounded by individuals who are dependent on him. He has the power to bless, ignore or punish them. He can "make their day."

---

*"I shall pass through this world but once.*
*If, therefore, there be any kindness I can show,*
*or any good thing I can do, let me do it now:*
*let me not defer it or neglect it,*
*for I shall not pass this way again."*
***Etienne de Grellet***

---

Many of us could be described as modern-day Boazes. Individuals with pressing needs surround us too. Some look to us for food and clothing, but usually these are not their most urgent needs. More often their hunger pangs are the longing for acceptance and affirmation, for protection and guidance. They are looking for handouts to feed their inner life. The modern-day Boaz recognizes that hunger and generously shares personal resources to satisfy the soul and spirit.

Gracious people make a difference in others' lives. They are God's agents of transformation.

Bart caught a glimpse of this one day as he was thinking about his family relationships. He attended a seminar at which I was describing how vital touch is to our lives. I related how well-fed infants in an orphanage mysteriously died for no apparent reason. As researchers sought for answers, they realized that these little babies were never picked up, caressed or hugged. A plan was implemented to provide each child with personal loving attention. The death rate changed drastically. They had discovered that a God-given need had been neglected. The effect on the infants was dramatic.

Bart thought about his children. Their arguing and fighting had troubled him. He also realized that too often he was busy with activities and rarely spent personal time with them individually—laughing with them, hugging them or telling what he admired about them. So he decided on a plan of action to touch their lives in these ways.

---

*"One kind word can warm three winter months."*
***Japanese proverb***

---

He noticed the difference right away. Their negative behaviors reduced noticeably. The children seemed more at peace with themselves and each other. A week or so later he approached me with a big grin on his face. Then he expressed how grateful he was that he had rediscovered something he'd lost. "I realize my children depend on me to fill their emotional tanks," he said. "They are counting on my warmth and affirmation of them to keep them healthy."

Our needs are a part of our Lord's wonderful design. *Needs are God-given receptors for love.* God created all of us with the same basic needs, but some of us live in environments that are more abundant in meeting those needs. Through no fault of their own, some children grow up in homes that are so love-starved that their need for affection or affirmation is rarely met. Others are blessed with parents who are generous with hugs and compliments that fill the child's emotional tank to the brim. Some adults work in vocations that are fulfilling, whereas others dread going to work because it is so boring.

We would encourage you to never see your God-created

needs as weaknesses; see them as the channels God uses to express his love to you. In fact, individuals who have no sense of need have no connecting point to God or others to receive love. They are self-sufficient islands.

Boaz's workers were well aware of their needs, and Boaz found joy in filling their tanks. By our Lord's loving design Ruth "happened" to be in Boaz's field that day when he stopped by to visit his workers. And so Ruth's life was changed when she encountered a man of grace. Though the story is about Ruth, Boaz's grace extends beyond her. Watch this man and you'll see that whenever he's on the scene, he communicates a care for others and a desire to be used of the Lord to express God's love.

**Grace Beyond My Prejudices**

Ruth had accompanied her mother-in-law, Naomi, to Bethlehem. She chose to be with this woman she had grown to love. She believed that she had a greater future in the presence of godly Naomi than by staying in her ungodly homeland. So her love had caused her to come to this strange, new land. But this would not be an easy transition.

Ruth arrives in Bethlehem a very vulnerable woman. She comes with only what she can carry on her back. She has no profession. She has no father or husband to protect her. She has no property. She arrives with an aging, bitter mother-in-law, whom Ruth loves dearly. But Naomi can offer little more than companionship. Though Ruth is a woman of great inner strength, she is still in a risky situation.

To grasp Ruth's situation you have to understand the Jewish culture of that day. Ruth had three strikes against her. First, she was a Gentile—a non-Jew—in a Jewish culture. The Jewish people knew that they were a chosen, covenant people who had found favor with the Lord. Many took fierce pride in this unique bond and believed that they were significantly different from the other nations. Old Testament prophets spoke of the Gentiles as enemies of God's people. They were considered pagans and were excluded from Jewish life. So it would not be uncommon for a non-Jew to be treated in a demeaning, uncaring and insensitive manner.

Strike two! Ruth was not only a Gentile, she was also from the land of Moab. The Moabites were descendants of Moab, the son of an incestuous relationship between Lot and his oldest daughter (Genesis 19:30-39). Israelites who took pride in their select heritage would look upon a Moabite with a prejudiced eye. You definitely didn't want your fine Jewish son to associate with a Moabite woman! So when Ruth entered Bethlehem's gates, she would encounter men and women who considered her spiritually defiled.

Strike three! Ruth was a woman. Most Jewish men didn't treat women as equals. Women did not have the rights that men did. More often they were considered property to be possessed. A daughter could be sold into slavery, becoming another man's property.

Add to this the fact that Ruth was a widow. Though the Old Testament law made provision for Jewish widows, Ruth would not qualify because she was an outsider, a stranger. This left her in a vulnerable position with no rights, no protection and no security. Even the fact that she was a barren widow—never having had children was also a cultural stigma against her.

Realistically Ruth's future looked very bleak. What man would want her? What was the likelihood that anyone would notice her or befriend her?

You cannot help but be impressed with Boaz's gracious spirit. He seemed to be unaffected by the cultural prejudices and mores that surround him. They hadn't penetrated his life. In fact, one of his most attractive features was his capacity to see beyond the outward rules and regulations and treat other people with dignity and respect. I know of no other Old Testament man who relates to a woman in this spirit of grace.

And men like that are needed to radiate our Lord's loving heart today.

So today Ruth chooses to work in the field that belonged to Boaz. It is a choice that will change her life. When Boaz arrives to interact with his workers, she is busy gathering whatever grain she can find. He sees Ruth following behind his reapers and asks his foreman about her.

Boaz is our Lord's personal ambassador to Ruth. He reaches out to her with God's arms of love. In this initial contact he welcomes her to his field. (And beyond that, it's obvious that he is welcoming her into his life.) He tells her that she will be protected; the workers have been instructed not to molest her in any way. He invites her to refresh herself with the water supply that is provided for the workers.

The fieldworkers who are watching this event are probably not surprised at Boaz's actions. After all, they know the caliber of man he is—perhaps many of them have been on the receiving end of his grace! But Ruth is struck profoundly by such unexpected grace. Her words and actions communicate the spirit of her amazement and gratitude. Her bowing down to the ground tells us that she believes people see her as an inferior. Her words reinforce this conviction. "Why have I found such favor in your eyes that you notice me—a foreigner?" Ruth utters (Ruth 2:10). Can you hear the message behind her words? "I'm an outsider. I don't have any rights or privileges. Why are you treating me with such undeserved kindness. I don't understand what's going on here, but I'm deeply grateful."

But there's more; Boaz isn't finished. He blesses her in the name of the Lord. "May the LORD repay what you have done. May you be richly rewarded by the LORD, the God of Israel, under whose wings you have come to take refuge" (Ruth 2:12). What joy these words must have brought to her heart, hearing a Jewish man pray God's blessing on her, an outsider. Before arriving in Bethlehem Ruth had confessed loyalty to Jehovah, the God of the Jews. Now Boaz affirms Jehovah's love and care for this needy woman. It's as though he confirms God's loving acceptance of her into the family of faith. "You have become one of us. Receive the blessing."

One writer has summarized Boaz's impact on Ruth in these words: "The Moabite shut out by the law is admitted by grace, and Ruth not only finds free grace but complete rest in Boaz."[3]

---

*"Kindness in words creates confidence.*
*Kindness in thinking creates profoundness.*
*Kindness in giving creates love."*
***Lao-tzu***

---

An attitude of grace transforms how we think about others. It transforms our relationships with them in distinction to what family and societal prejudices teach. Just as Ruth is seeing Jehovah's love expressed in Boaz's words and actions, we can model the tender, loving heart of our heavenly Father in the same way.

Ours is a world of prejudice. Probably none of us are immune from some form of discrimination. We live with barriers of social status, wealth, ethnic or family heritage, ability—the list goes on. We become weary of the constant emphasis on how different men and women are, with the implication that we can never understand each other, we can't have common interests, we can't work together, ad infinitum. Boaz reminds us that we have common roots that give us a solid basis for joyful relationships.

Large numbers of women today still feel the sting of prejudice that men often communicate to them. In countless ways men have communicated a sense of superiority over women, leaving deep wounds in their lives. Abuse comes in many forms, some subtle, some obvious, but either form leaves hurt.

That's why women are attracted to men who exhibit a Boaz kind of grace. That's why we challenge men to excel in this godly trait. In no sense is it exclusive to men, but when men embody the spirit of grace, they build strong bridges of relationship with women, not only modeling the heart of our Lord but revealing the heart of godly men. It's not exclusive to men, but men should lead in it and model it before women.

**Grace Guards**

I've already described Ruth's vulnerable condition. She can be easily exploited. Boaz, though, recognizes her desperate, defenseless condition. In the opening scene when the two of them meet, Boaz immediately lets her know that he has made provision for her physical safety. "I have told the men not to touch you," he says (Ruth 2:9). What comfort this must have brought to her heart. Evil men must have thought about how they could exploit this woman and get away with it. If one chose to rape her, who would defend her? After all, she was a foreigner, a Gentile and a Moabitess.

Knowing that Boaz had warned men about their conduct around Ruth must have given her a strong sense of security. But it also told her something about Boaz and his intentions. If he wouldn't let others take advantage of her, she had reason to believe that he wouldn't do so either. Now she knew that she could come to the field each day and work without worrying about sexual harassment.

This gracious man provides a second kind of protection. After the noontime lunch break he has a word with his workers. He tells them, "Even if she gathers among the sheaves, don't embarrass her. Rather, pull out some stalks for her from the bundles and leave them for her to pick up, and don't rebuke her" (Ruth 2:15).

What's happening here?

Ruth came into this field as an outsider, not an employee. The Jewish law provided for the poor by allowing them to pick up grain that the reapers had overlooked as they passed through the fields. Usually this was a sparse picking that would keep a person alive. Ruth would not be allowed to gather *among* the sheaves because that would be where the abundant grain was and where the reapers would be working.

Boaz says two things to his workers. First, he instructs them that they are not to say anything that would embarrass Ruth. No rude or insensitive comments about her status. No chiding her because she came too close to the sheaves. Second, he tells the workers that they are to *purposely* leave grain behind that will give abundance to Ruth as she gleans after them.

These actions on Boaz's part demonstrate his commitment to provide emotional protection for Ruth. It's one thing to make sure that she is physically safe. It's another to be certain that she doesn't have to face ridicule, embarrassment and demeaning actions from others. *Women deeply appreciate men who protect their emotional state.* Boaz affirmed Ruth in his own conduct, and he made certain that others knew that he expected that of them too.

Several years ago I was the pastor of a small church family. One evening the men were meeting for a time of support, encouragement and instruction. I spoke to the men something like this:

> We are called to be men of God. One way we can demonstrate this is by treating the women of this fellowship with courtesy, respect and dignity. Many have experienced forms of degradation and abuse in past relationships. Let's make a covenant that we will always affirm and strengthen these women. Let's agree that we will never use sarcasm or women-bashing jokes toward them.

The men lived by that covenant, and the Lord formed a special community of men and women who affirmed and strengthened each other. This is the spirit of Boaz lived out today. (Interestingly enough, it also freed the women to relate to the men because they didn't have to be guarded or defensive for fear of being abused.)

Boaz shows us a third kind of protection. Later in this account Ruth follows Naomi's counsel and goes at night to the threshing floor to seek Boaz's protection. (The threshing floor was an open, hard surface where bundled grain would be separated from the straw and chaff.) The procedure follows a custom of that day in which Ruth could ask Boaz to be her kinsman-redeemer. He was asleep at the threshing floor when Ruth quietly approached him, laid down at his feet and covered herself with a part of the blanket that covered him. Later he awoke and realized that someone was at his feet. In the conversation that followed, Ruth makes the request that he redeem her according to Jewish custom. This includes redeeming another's lost property, possibly redeeming another from slavery and redeeming another's lost legacy by providing an heir. (We shall examine the role of a kinsman-redeemer more fully in chapter eleven.) Boaz agrees to pursue the matter.

Early in the morning Boaz instructs Ruth to leave before others awake. "Don't let it be known that a woman came to the threshing floor," he says. In this action Boaz is protecting Ruth's reputation. He doesn't want rumors started that this woman had acted in some inappropriate manner. He is protecting her from the shame of gossip or misinterpreted motives.

A man who lovingly protects a woman's reputation is a joy to behold. Some men are looking for opportunities to take advantage of women and then brag about their conquests. Men who follow Jesus Christ have a different code of ethics. They know that they are called to guard women, not use them for their own gratification.

**Grace Speaks Kindly**

My wife, Winnie, has always been a fan of Winnie-the-Pooh. These stories are well-known to our family. In one incident Winnie-the-Pooh is walking in the Hundred "Aker" Wood one late morning. As he walks, he thinks about whom he could visit. (At an appropriate time just prior to lunch!) At the time this thought occurs to him, he is crossing a stream, so he pauses, sits down on a stone in the middle of the stream and ponders this urgent decision, "Who shall I visit?"

"I think I'll go see Tigger," he thinks. "No," he says, dismissing that thought.

"Owl then!" he thinks. "No, Owl uses big words, hard-to-understand words," he decides.

Suddenly the light flashes in his mind. "I know! I think I'll go see Rabbit. I like Rabbit. Rabbit uses encouraging words like, 'How's about lunch?' and 'Help yourself, Pooh!' Yes, I think I'll go see Rabbit."

Pooh Bear is drawn to Rabbit because Rabbit is gracious with his words. And Ruth is drawn to Boaz because he is a man gracious in his speech.

---

*"Wise sayings often fall on barren ground;*
*but a kind word is never thrown away."*
***Sir Arthur Helps***

---

And we are drawn to others who speak with the spirit of grace. People are drawn to men and women who know how to speak from a heart of grace. We can learn much of this as we examine the relationship between Ruth and Boaz.

Everything about Boaz's speech is warm and affirming. In our first glimpse of the man he greets his workers with "The LORD be with you." Then as we are privileged to listen in on his conversation with Ruth, we feel something of what she must have felt—a woman with no standing being spoken to with warmth, kindness and courtesy.

Ruth specifically mentions the powerful impact his words have had on her. She says, "You have given me comfort and have spoken kindly to your servant—though I do not have the standing of one of your servant girls" (Ruth 2:13). "Spoken kindly" has the meaning of "spoken to the heart." Ruth is saying, "Your words have spoken to my heart. They have encouraged me and given me comfort."

How powerful words are when they speak to our heart! When they strengthen us in our weakness. When they impart peace amid turmoil. When they build us up when others have been tearing us down. When they refresh our weary spirit.

The writer of Proverbs reminds us that "reckless words pierce like a sword, but the tongue of the wise brings healing" (Proverbs 12:18). And later he says that "the tongue has the power of life and death" (Proverbs 18:21). What powerful statements! And we know from experience that they are true. We've all felt the sting of sarcasm, mockery or putdown jokes at our expense. We've also felt the pleasant summer breeze of words that refresh, fill us with hope and leave us feeling special.

The New Testament has a parallel passage that urges us to be men and women who speak grace-filled words. In Ephesians 4:29 we read, "Let no unwholesome word proceed from your mouth, but only such a word as is good for edification according to the need of the moment, that it may give grace to those who hear"(NASB). This is a powerful thought that the apostle Paul is urging on his hearers. Can you hear him saying, "Your words can communicate grace. They can be *God's words* to someone else"?

---

*"A great many people think they are thinking,*
*when they are merely rearranging their prejudices."*
***William James***

---

It's true. Our words can build others up. (By the way, the word *edification* was used in Paul's day to describe how a carpenter would build a house. It's a construction word.) Our hearers can feel strengthened, refreshed or affirmed by our words. As men and women who are empowered and led by God's Spirit, our conversations can literally be a means whereby the Spirit communicates his grace to the one who is listening to us. That's why the next statement Paul makes is "And do not grieve the Holy Spirit of God" (Ephesians 4:30). Do you see what he's driving at? When we are not speaking to others in a grace-full manner, we deny God's Spirit the opportunity to encourage or strengthen someone else.

We think that's a powerful truth. We think it's exciting to know that we can be our Lord's ambassador of good news to those around us. We get to speak his words of refreshment and hope to those who are downtrodden, discouraged or defeated. And Ruth's response to Boaz's words reminds us how others will be affected by our words: "You have given me comfort and spoken to my heart—though I don't deserve it."

**Grace: The Crown Jewel of Relationships**

Ruth entered Boaz's field that morning, little realizing that the man she would meet there would change her life. History was being made that day. When she entered the field, life seemed harsh and her future looked bleak. But when she met a man of grace, she was filled with hope. That's the power of grace. It signals that someone cares. Someone is reaching out to me. Someone notices my plight.

The grace of our loving heavenly Father has filled our lives, giving us a solid hope. Now we have the privilege of sharing that grace to those around us. As grace-filled men and women relate to each other, they communicate in tangible ways the value placed on each other's lives. And we bear witness that our lives are significant to another person.

We live in a throwaway culture. Sadly many people move through numerous throwaway relationships. The beauty of someone who prizes and protects relationships is obvious. Our challenge is to be daily renewed and refreshed in our Lord's grace and then pass it on to others.

**What's Here for Us?**

1. Would your friends consider you more of a "truth person" or a "grace person"? How does it affect your relationships?

2. What troubling prejudices do you observe among Christians?

3. In what way are you prejudiced toward persons of the opposite sex?

4. Discuss the idea that grace prepares the soil of a person's heart to receive truth. What are the implications of this concept?

5. Why might it be important for men to be strong in expressing grace toward women?

6. Using a Bible concordance, look up the word *grace* and discover what further insights you can gain on its importance and application.

7. Think of one person who needs to experience God's grace more fully. What could you do to express that *through your life*?

8. How fully have you experienced God's grace? In what ways has it liberated you from sin, defeat and failure?

9. What more do you want to understand about being a man or woman of grace?

# 4

# Submission
## *Serving or Suffering?*

MENTION THE WORD *SUBMISSION* TO MOST WOMEN TODAY and you've probably "pushed their button." They're likely to cringe or make a sarcastic comeback. The idea of a submissive spirit has been terribly distorted and abused, leading to overwhelming contempt for the concept. Feminists and women's rights advocates would have us believe that submissive women are weak women, quietly accepting a life of servitude and slavery. Yet God's plan for submission is the complete opposite—it's freeing rather than binding. More important, God's plan extends beyond the male-female relationship. Biblically both men *and* women are to exhibit the inner spirit of submission. First Peter 5:5 exhorts, "Young men, in the same way be submissive to those who are older." And Ephesians 5:22 encourages men and women to "submit to one another out of reverence for Christ."

The book of Ruth paints a beautiful picture of submission—not so obviously in the relationship between Ruth and Boaz—but in the relationship between Ruth and Naomi. The beauty of this relationship is that it displays submission as an inner quality that has nothing to do with gender. Rather, it is the fruit of godliness.

Scripture reveals how Ruth, a strong and determined woman, repeatedly yields to Naomi's authority and wisdom. "Don't urge me to leave you or to turn back from you. Where you go I will go, and where you stay I will stay. Your people will be my people and your God my God. . . . May the LORD deal with me, be it ever so severely, if anything but death separates you and me" (Ruth 1:16-17). By swearing this to God, Ruth not only affirms her commitment to Naomi, but she demonstrates her submission to Naomi's God—a major commitment for a Moabitess.

You may be thinking, *Well, of course Ruth was committed to Naomi. She didn't have anywhere else to go. And they probably got along like best friends. Now if you only knew the people I have to live with* . . . But read the book of Ruth a little closer. Naomi was no Mary Sunshine! She was bitter (even changing her name to "Mara," which means bitter); she felt as if God's hand was against her; she described herself as empty and afflicted. Ruth must have realized that it would be no picnic to stay with this woman, yet she willingly did. In spite of their circumstances Ruth trusted Naomi completely. "I will do whatever you say" (Ruth 3:5).

---

*"Submission is the inescapable path to power that lasts."*
***Howard Butt***

---

**The Willingness (and Wisdom) to Yield**

Today how many of us (both men *and* women) are involved in

relationships in which we could honestly and wholeheartedly declare, "I will do whatever you say"? Is it hard for you to submit yourself to another—regardless of gender? As our culture urges us to be more and more self-reliant, we become less and less willing to rely on the wisdom and experience of others. It's likely that most people have a very inaccurate view of what submission looks like in a relationship. So let's set the record straight and take a closer look at what submission looks like.

*Submission is give and take.* A new department store recently opened near Jody's home. The road to the new store had to join the road that leads to a large outlet mall; so the planners designed an intricate roundabout in which drivers going to the department store must yield to the mall traffic. The large, yellow yield sign clues drivers into the fact that there will be some give and take at this intersection—or there will be trouble! You might think of submission as sort of a yield sign in a relationship. Just as there are appropriate times and situations in which we must yield to other drivers, there are times and situations in which we need to "yield" to the wisdom of others. Their position, knowledge or experience gives them the "right of way," and we would be foolish to cut in.

To better understand this give and take, let's return to the story of Ruth and Naomi. It's interesting to note that *the two women actually have opportunity to submit to each other.* In the beginning of the story, when Ruth commits herself to staying with Naomi, Naomi submits to Ruth's will. "When Naomi realized that Ruth was determined to go with her, she stopped urging her" (Ruth 1:18). Perhaps Naomi was inwardly relieved to have the company. Or maybe she realized she was fighting an uphill battle. It could be that she knew that Ruth was right. Whatever the reason, Naomi knew when to humbly say, "Okay, we'll do it your way." She wasn't too proud to give in to this younger woman.

In the same way, Ruth wasn't so headstrong that she ignored the advice of an older, wiser woman. Maybe Naomi's recommendations made Ruth uncomfortable. Perhaps she thought, *You want me to do* what? *I could get into real trouble that way!* Yet following Naomi's counsel Ruth found the best place to glean and an appropriate way to respond to Boaz. When Ruth "did everything her mother-in-law told her to do" (Ruth 3:6), the result was always favorable.

We believe that because these women loved and cared for each other, they were willing to submit to each other. *The ability to express healthy love frees us to submit.* Naomi and Ruth's relationship showed a balanced sense of give and take. Neither woman sought to be the "head honcho" or the "boss." Instead, they looked for ways to care for each other and provide for each other's needs.

---

*"Submission doesn't whittle you down, it builds you up."*
***Howard Butt***

---

Our relationships need that same balance today. Remember the yield sign mentioned earlier? One key element of that intersection is that all drivers must be tuned in to what is happening around them. Drivers who barrel through with the attitude of "I have the right of way so you'd better just watch out," run the risk of being hit by another driver who may also be in a hurry or may have missed the sign. Similarly, if we charge through life with the attitude of "I'm in charge! No one can tell *me* what to do!" we run the risk of heartbreaking conflict. Submission is give and take. Sometimes you will have the right of way, but there will be many appropriate times to yield.

Notice, too, that when we exhibit a submissive spirit, we more likely encourage it in others. But road rage is often initiated because someone doesn't practice courtesy toward another. "Get out of my way!" makes the other person more likely to respond with "I'll show you!" Just as pride ignites pride, submission ignites submission.

*Submission is servanthood, not slavery.* One of the greatest misperceptions about submission is that it makes us someone else's slave. "I'll just be a doormat for him to walk all over." "She'll boss me around, telling me what to do like I'm some sort of slave." But this is clearly *not* God's plan for submission. *God's plan was demonstrated by Jesus.* "Who, being in very nature God, did not consider equality with God something to be grasped, but made himself nothing, taking the very nature of a servant, being made in human likeness. And being found in appearance as a man, he humbled himself and became obedient to death—even death on a cross!" (Philippians 2:6-8). Although Jesus, God's Son, willingly submitted to humanity—that is, becoming human—note that he did not give up his deity. While a slave is considered property, a servant is simply one who serves. Humanity (or human form) never "owned" Jesus (as demonstrated by his resurrection), but Jesus submitted to becoming human in order to serve.

A submissive heart is one that desires to serve and help others. Submission doesn't mean that you give up your identity to be at the beck and call of another. Submission simply requires you to put the needs of others before those of yourself. Ruth and Naomi both display a servant's heart. After her husband and sons have died, Naomi thinks of her daughters-in-law. "Go back, each of you, to your mother's home. May the LORD show kindness to you, as you have shown to your dead and to me. May the LORD grant that each of you will find rest in the home of another husband" (Ruth 1: 8-9).

It's evident that Naomi had become attached to her daughters-in-law. They provided her with friendship and support. But in thinking of their best interests Naomi gives the best advice that she can, setting aside her own needs—for companionship and perhaps income—to offer what would be best for the two younger women. Ironically Ruth turns the situation around and offers herself in service to Naomi! Ruth provides companionship, food and a home for Naomi. Her love for the older woman is so great that Ruth goes out of her way to serve and provide.

---

*"Rebelling reflects your insecurity;*
*submitting, you show your calm sure sense of strength."*
***Howard Butt***

---

What a powerful example for us! Their mutual submission creates an environment where each blesses the other. (It's impossible to improve on our Lord's plan!)

A servant's heart is impossible to hide. It shows in everything that person does or says. My daughter Amy has a true servant's heart. Amy loves to take a homemade pie and a dish of lasagna to a family with a new baby. She delights in caring for a shut-in or cleaning house for someone who is unable to get up and around. She willingly gives her time and energy to those who have none. We will be the first to note that people are drawn to Amy—it's a treat to be in her home! A servant's heart is so endearing because it is characterized by things like willingness, joy and delight. Therein lies the difference between being a servant and a slave. While a slave trudges to his task, a servant delights in helping another. While a slave grumbles about his or her duties, a servant sings as he or she serves.

A submissive heart is a servant's heart. It is a heart that draws others in, attracting them to the joy inside.

---

*" 'Freedom' for many in modern society means the freedom from being told what to do."*
***Stephen Clark***

---

*Submission allows another to lead out of his or her strengths.* About eight months ago I faced the truth that I needed more serious upper-body exercise than walking would provide, so I signed on the dotted line and paid my dues at a local health club. One of the immediate benefits was the services of a personal trainer, John. I had in my mind what I wanted to do, but John said, "No, that's not how you begin training. Let me show you the proper way."

So we began with warm-up exercises. (I had expected that I'd just jump on the weightlifting machines and work out until I was hot, tired and sweaty.) Then John said, "You now need to do a series of stretching activities." So I stretched. (Ah. Now I get to the heavy-duty stuff.) But even when we moved to the exercise machines, John had a plan that differed from what I had expected; so again I submitted to my trainer's knowledge and skill.

Now, months later, I enjoy working out regularly. In addition, I have the confidence that I'm doing it properly because I was willing to do what John told me to do. By submitting to John's strengths, I've been very pleased with my progress.

By submitting to the wisdom and expertise of an experienced trainer, I have been able to become healthier. I could have jogged, climbed or lifted weights using my own set of guidelines, but it wouldn't have been the wisest or most effective use of time. In order to achieve my goal, I had to follow the guidelines set by an expert.

It's likely that most people you interact with have certain areas of expertise or giftedness. Think of these gifts as tools in a toolbox. God has blessed each person with a toolbox of specially designed tools called gifts, talents and abilities. Each person's toolbox looks a little different from the next. You may have tools such as hospitality, encouraging words or even humor. Another may have a toolbox filled with financial understanding, a keen business sense or an eye for details. When facing a dilemma, a submissive heart will allow the person with the right tools to fix the problem!

---

*"My role has been to help other people look good, and I love doing that."*
***Bill Gaither***

---

Ruth was a foreigner who knew little if anything about social customs in Bethlehem. Naomi had just the right tools for the situation—family connections and a wealth of cultural understanding. By allowing Naomi to lead out of her strengths, Ruth was able to assimilate into the culture and respond appropriately to Boaz's words and actions. Rather than attempting to lead out of her weakness (and thereby become lost), Ruth submitted to Naomi and found success at every turn.

Think for a moment about your toolbox. List the tools that you might find there. What things do you enjoy? In what areas do you excel? What brings you the greatest joy in life? When people come to you for advice, what type of help are they usually seeking? Now, think of those whom you interact with most often. List the items you would find in their toolboxes. These lists are simple reminders of our strengths and the strengths of others.

In 1805 two famous explorers named Lewis and Clark discovered that their "toolboxes" were lacking some vital equipment. In their quest for the Pacific Ocean they ran into a stumbling block somewhere near modern-day North Dakota. As they were preparing to travel west from the Dakotas, the famous explorers realized that they needed a guide—someone who knew the lay of the land—and an interpreter who could help them communicate with the various tribes they would encounter. These important men submitted their world-famous journey—and ultimately their lives—to the wisdom of a Native American woman named Sacajawea. The knowledge and skill of this former slave proved invaluable to the expedition. If Lewis and Clark had tried to continue on their own knowledge, it's likely that the expedition would have failed. Their willingness to submit was paramount to their success.

When *we* wholeheartedly submit to the strengths of others, we keep from blazing a wandering, meandering trail through life. When we allow others to use their tools, the result is a strong foundation and a solid faith. Without a submissive heart we are ultimately weak, lost and terribly alone.

**In the Driver's Seat**

As I pointed out earlier in this chapter, it can be hard to submit to another. Ours is a culture that values independence: holding up the entrepreneur who made a fortune on his own, lauding the single parent who raised three children single-handedly, pushing our children to be more self-sufficient at a younger age. Although there's nothing wrong with independence, we are often led to believe that it is a sign of weakness to depend upon or submit to another. Yet a person—male or female—who refuses to submit, faces a lonely and frustrating life. Let's explore a few reasons why.

*Lack of submission creates a lack of trust in others.* Looking back at the relationship between Ruth and Naomi, it's evident that Ruth completely trusted Naomi's judgment. Ruth had spent time with Naomi, she knew her mother-in-law well enough to believe that the older woman knew the appropriate behavior and customs. Perhaps during the time Ruth was married to Mahlon (Naomi's son), she caught glimpses of Naomi's character. Thus Ruth was willing to put her future into Naomi's hands and follow her directions. Just as submission requires trust, a continuous *lack of submission* breeds a sense of distrust in others.

To better understand how this works, think back to the example of the yield sign. Imagine that you are a driver who never yields to other cars. You barrel into the lane with the attitude that "I was here first, and this is my lane!" How would others respond to you? It's likely that they'd honk, shout or maybe even offer a few obscene gestures! Your car might even get hit once in a while. With such a reception you'll begin to distrust and dislike *all* drivers. "Boy, drivers today are sure grouchy. All they do is lay on that horn and yell!" Even when you're not at a yield sign, you might assume that they're all out to get you.

Our hearts are much the same. When we barrel through life with the attitude that "I can make all of my own decisions," we offend and alienate those around us. They may protest, offer advice or simply shake their heads—and "accidents" are inevitable. Hearts will be broken and relationships crushed. A heart that refuses to yield becomes hardened and callused to the outside world. It becomes diseased with distrust and suspicion.

*Lack of submission creates an illusion that "I have to be in control."* Our culture resonates with the word *I.* We read magazines with titles like *Self* and *Moi.* Their covers tout articles such as "Taking Control of Your Life," "15 Ways to Get What You Want . . . Every Time!" or "Make Him Listen to You." Women in particular are bombarded with messages about being in control of their lives, their homes, their careers and their relationships.

What a detour we've taken from God's original plan! In Genesis 1:28 God speaks to Adam *and* Eve. "God blessed them and said to them, 'Be fruitful and increase in number; fill the earth and subdue it. Rule over the fish of the sea and the birds of the air and over every living creature that moves on the ground.' " God's plan was for Adam and Eve to work together as a team, united in accomplishing his purposes. God's plan was for men and women to be a team, and any athlete will tell you that teamwork means submitting to the wisdom and expertise of a coach or coaching staff. An athlete who tries to run the game his or her own way is very likely to drag the team away from victory.

---

*"One of the things I learned from working with the Dallas Cowboys is the importance of the team. When you are on a team, you play off the strengths of your teammates. You don't tackle the guys who wear the same color uniforms."*

***Howard Hendricks***

---

Further, a controlling heart that refuses to submit will wear down. How tiring—physically and emotionally—it is to be in control all the time! Even the "strongest" will buckle under the pressure to do it all perfectly all the time. Many years ago the Wakefield clan took a month-long trip across the United States. I bought a van large enough to comfortably seat the seven family members for the long driving stretches that we would make. Amy and Joel, my two oldest children, who were nearing college age, were excited to share in the driving. But what if I had said, "This is a new van, and I don't trust anyone else to drive it. I'll be doing all the driving on this trip"? By taking complete control I would have been tired, weary from the long hours of driving. I would have missed the opportunity to wholeheartedly take in the view as we cruised past beautiful mountains, streams and farmland. I would have given up the chance to sit in the backseat and talk with the younger children, getting to know them better. And I would have sent a clear message to my older kids: "I don't trust you."

*A lack of submission often leads to poor decisions or results because it doesn't use others' strengths to the best advantage.* Several months ago Jody and her husband noticed that they had a leaky faucet in the bathtub. After consulting a few "do-it-yourself" manuals, they tackled the job with great enthusiasm . . . that quickly turned to frustration and fatigue. The plumbing in their older house had been poorly maintained, making a "simple" task seemingly impossible. Rather than fixing the faucet, the previous owners had merely used large amounts of powerful glue to stop the drip. Not wanting to make the same mistake, Jody and Erik called in a friend with a good knowledge of plumbing. After a few hours the leak was fixed—the right way.

How do you handle those "leaky faucets" in life? When faced with a problem, do you tackle it yourself or do you find others who can help? Do you patch up conflicts haphazardly or seek experts who can get it done the right way? Lack of submission often results in poor solutions simply because we won't look to the experts. Again, let's look to God's plan. James 3:17 advises, "But the wisdom that comes from heaven is first of all pure; then peace-loving, considerate, submissive, full of mercy and good fruit, impartial and sincere." Godly wisdom is submissive. Submitting to another doesn't indicate ignorance or stupidity—rather it shows wisdom and discernment. A submissive heart knows when to call in the expert and fully rely on his or her understanding.

Ultimately we all must submit to the wisdom and power of God, trusting in him to guide us through life. We can draw great insight from James 4:7: "Submit yourselves, then, to God. Resist the devil and he will flee from you." Without submitting ourselves to God and allowing him to guide us, we will be powerless to stand against Satan's schemes. Only a fool would willingly fight that battle alone, especially with the knowledge that God is the only one who can win it. On a different level, we are fools when pride keeps us from seeking (and heeding) the counsel of the wise.

**Avoid the Temptation**

One of the barriers that keeps us from submitting to others is the tendency to think that we have to be in charge of everything. Another is that we refuse to recognize that the Lord may have a different plan or procedure than we prefer. Thus we have to avoid the temptation to step in and take charge when someone else is responsible to oversee or lead.

This raises the question of whom we trust and whom we follow. If submission is a biblical principle under God's sovereign leadership, then we always have to view our relationships with others in this light.

We cannot talk about submission without talking about trust. Often our Lord asks us to allow another person to do something in his or her own way—a way that is uncomfortable or different from our preferred way. If we are placed in a situation in which we are to submit to another person, we have to trust our heavenly Father that he will guide the other person and that he will care for us. It also means that we free the other person to respond to our Lord's leading and not our control.

**It's Tool Time**

We've defined submission and attempted to banish many of the myths and stigma that surround the concept of submissiveness. We've also explored the heartache and grief that arise when we continually refuse to submit. But what happens when we wisely yield to another? How does submission affect our relationships? Does having a submissive heart allow us to grow spiritually? Our culture is so devoid of positive examples, many of us have no idea what submission looks like in a relationship, let alone comprehend it's lasting effects. Read on to discover how your relationships today can be nurtured through an attitude of submission.

*Submission allows others' strengths to emerge and flourish.* When Naomi's husband and sons died, emptiness and hopelessness must have overwhelmed her. For years her identity was found in her role as wife, then as a mother. Now she felt useless. "'Call me Mara, because the Almighty has made my life very bitter. I went away full, but the LORD has brought me back empty. Why call me Naomi? The LORD has afflicted me; the Almighty has brought misfortune upon me' " (Ruth 1:20-21). From her attitude we can guess that she didn't see herself as a woman with any strengths—or tools—to share. Ruth changed that through her submissive heart. In Judah, Naomi suddenly had tremendous value as a guide and counselor for Ruth. She had wisdom, cultural knowledge and family connections she could share. When Ruth asked for and submitted to Naomi's advice, Naomi's heart was changed. Her bitterness was replaced with joy and hope. Her strengths were suddenly evident and useful.

Remember the toolbox analogy? God has blessed every person with a full toolbox—but some people haven't even opened the lid to that box! One of Jody's supervisors recently approached her with a new and challenging project that involved scriptwriting. "I've tried to get the script right, and I've realized this is just not my area of giftedness. But I believe *you* can do it," the woman said. "I've seen your work for the past several years, and I honestly believe that you have a gift for this. I feel confident in handing this project over to you." As a supervisor this woman had the wisdom to submit to someone else's expertise. For Jody it was an exciting opportunity to stretch and grow in a skill she truly did enjoy. The project was finished in a timely manner, under budget and was done well. Through her submissive heart the supervisor not only got the job done but encouraged the skills of her employee.

Think back to the list you made of people's tools. When can you step back and rely on such tools? How can you encourage and develop those skills? What will be the long-term impact of having that toolbox available to you? Through a healthy sense of submission individuals can strengthen their relationships by strengthening those to whom they relate. People will begin to see you as an encourager, someone who brings out the best in them. As a result, relationships will be deeper and more fulfilling, since both members are growing.

*Submission creates balance.* We began this chapter by investigating the give-and-take nature of submission. When that give and take is ongoing, a beautiful sense of balance and harmony pervades the relationship. The participants in the relationship become a unified team. One of my students put it this way:

> In my own life, I have often been irritated when my wife has asked me to help her with tasks which seemed to be more of a woman's chore. After all, I don't ask her to help tend to the lawn, trim the trees, or repair appliances. Now I am realizing that when she asks for my assistance, she is not placing me in a subordinate role, but rather asking me to come alongside for support. The difference is very significant, and motivates me to be more willing to assist in these situations.

This man had come to understand a key element in any relationship—between coworkers, spouses or friends—and that is the concept of balance. Individuals need others to complement them. That was much of the reason God created Eve *for Adam.* Adam was incomplete without her. "The LORD God said, 'It is not good for the man to be alone. I will make a helper suitable for him.' . . . For this reason a man will leave his father and mother and be united to his wife, and they will become one flesh" (Genesis 2:18, 24).

Submission that follows God's definition and plan as laid out in Scripture enhances that sense of harmony and balance. That gentle give and take creates an almost tangible peace in any relationship. You'll note it in a work setting when supervisors aren't afraid to submit to the wisdom or advice of an employee. You can't miss it in a family when siblings learn to yield to each other's strengths. And it's undeniable in a marriage when husband and wife lean on each other for support, approaching life as a team.

---

*"Proper submission to godly leaders can bring purpose, peace and blessing: rebellion against godly authority can bring unrest and the disrupted life, missing God's best."*
***Bill Bright***

---

As Ruth submitted to Naomi, their relationship changed and took on a warmth and harmony as well. Ruth cared for Naomi and met her physical needs (Ruth 2:17). Naomi sheltered Ruth and provided her with advice (Ruth 2:23; 3:1-4). Just as Naomi gives Ruth a family through herself and her relations in Judah, Ruth gives Naomi a family through the birth of Obed. These two women discover the peace that comes from fully relying on each other. And their relationship settles into a calm sense of balance that is truly beautiful to the reader. Submission, that servant's heart, opened the doors for friendship to truly blossom.

*Submission communicates respect and appreciation.* In the first chapter of Ruth we see Naomi as empty and bitter. She is a woman who has been robbed of her status and position. Yet Ruth's actions and attitude restore Naomi's sense of self-worth in amazing ways. This is the power of a submissive heart.

Let's be certain not to confuse submission with flattery. The two are at opposite ends of the spectrum. Ruth didn't fawn over Naomi, telling her how wonderful and wise she was. It's doubtful that she even asked Naomi's advice in order to make Naomi feel better. Rather, Ruth's heart was sincere, and she wholeheartedly followed Naomi's guidance. False sincerity and a front of submission will never communicate respect. Instead, it will offend and alienate, building a wall of distrust. Submission must be sincere, with the intent to follow through completely.

A successful relationship requires the acknowledgment of respect on both sides. Without mutual respect and appreciation a relationship can be only a stunted, one-sided association. It can not grow or flourish, become richer and deeper, or develop into true friendship. That is why a submissive heart is such a key element in any relationship. By graciously submitting to the wisdom or will of another, we subconsciously convey the message "I trust and respect you. I'm willing to put myself under your guidance in this matter." Submission goes beyond spoken words or compliments and reaches into the heart of a person. What a simple way to develop a sense of trust in a relationship!

Today *submission* is a word that makes many people recoil with distaste. It has been misunderstood, misinterpreted and misused. However, God's plan for submission is rich and beautiful. By studying and putting biblical submission into action in our lives, we have the power to enrich our relationships and accentuate the strengths of those around us.

*To implement godly submission we must first throw away any preconceived notions or definitions*. Erase the picture of a toiling, beaten-down slave and replace it with an image of Christ. Take your cue from him and be bold enough to be a servant. Your relationships will never be the same again.

**What's Here for Us?**

1. What or who has shaped your understanding of submission?
2. How hard is it for you to submit yourself to another—regardless of gender?
3. What damage have you seen (or even caused) by not yielding to another?
4. Think of a specific time when you *did* submit to another. Who was it? What was the outcome?
5. What keeps you from serving with a submissive heart? (Take a moment and pray that God would remove this barrier to healthy relationships.)
6. Specifically, how can you envision your relationships being more healthy through your own submissive heart?
7. Jot a list of other people's "toolboxes." How does it feel to know that you have those tools available to you?

# 5

# Godliness

## *God's Beauty Reproduced*

YOU COULD CALL ME AND MY FRIEND SHERMAN "SOUL MATES." Until Sherman's company transferred him to the East Coast, the two of us would meet every Labor Day weekend at a family camp near Santa Cruz, California. From the beginning we were drawn together by similar values and goals, and especially because of our love for Jesus Christ.

One weekend Sherman's son, Tim, came with his family to spend a day with his parents. As Tim and I were enjoying lunch together, Tim began to describe the joy he experienced when he worked with wood. He has honed his skill to become a master craftsman. His specialty is making custom rocking chairs.

"You've designed this rocking chair yourself?" I asked him.

"Yes," Tim replied, "the design is very beautiful, and I'll only use the best wood. I want this to last for generations. You can't mass-produce this kind of rocking chair. It takes hours and hours to construct it, to sand it and to finish it properly. There are no shortcuts if it's to be a thing of beauty. Each chair is 'one of a kind.' "

I left the table not only in awe of Tim's refined craftsmanship but pondering those things that endure for generations as objects of beauty. My synapses began to zap as I made other connections. I envisioned godliness as our Lord's handcrafting our lives to become something of beauty that reflects the wisdom, skill and love of the Master Craftsman. A godly person is an expression of the heart of our Lord. He pours his energy into us, fashioning us into a reflection of who he is.

A person could look at Tim's rocking chair and see an expression of the talented man who made it. In like manner, people can look at us and see evidence of our Lord's creative activity as he transforms us into his image. The apostle Paul depicted this when he penned the words "And we, who with unveiled faces all reflect the Lord's glory, are being transformed into his likeness with ever-increasing glory, which comes from the Lord, who is the Spirit" (2 Corinthians 3:18).

Cal Thomas is a newspaper columnist. His youngest adult daughter sent him a Father's Day card. On the front were the following words: "I wonder if you realize how much of what I believe in comes from all you taught me and how much of what I am goes back to your love." Inside she had written the message: "You and Mom have been such wonderful role models. I hope one day you will really know the example that you have set for me and all of us kids. I am so thankful that God gave me a dad like you. . . . I love you Dad."

In reporting this incident Cal Thomas said, "No other Father's Day gift ever meant as much to me as that one. I carry it in my briefcase to remind me of the rewards of priorities."[1]

**Finding Someone to Follow**

Ruth's family tree sprouted from bad seed. The roots of the Moabite nation formed from an incestuous relationship between Abraham's nephew, Lot, and Lot's daughter. As the nation developed, they became enemies of Israel. They were an ungodly nation, worshiping their national idol, Chemosh, who was honored with child sacrifices (2 Kings 3:26-27). When the Israelites first encountered the Moab king, Balak, he tried to hire the prophet Balaam to curse Israel. When that tactic failed, he attempted to lure them into evil idolatry.

According to Deuteronomy 7:2, the children of Israel were instructed to destroy the Moabites. They were forbidden from making any peace treaties with them. So we can see that moving to Moab was not an act of godliness—definitely not an expression of trust in the Lord. In addition, the Jews were warned not to give sons or daughters in marriage to a Moabite family (Deuteronomy 7:3). Thus when Elimelech and Naomi sanctioned the marriage of their son to Ruth, it was in direct violation of God's commands.

So when Ruth married Naomi's son and became a part of this Jewish family, we are left to wonder what impression of godliness she received. Though Elimelech's name means "God is King," rather than trust God in hard times, he moved to an ungodly culture to escape difficult circumstances.

Even Naomi, Ruth's mother-in-law, cries out that her Lord is her adversary. As the two women enter Bethlehem, they encounter Naomi's old friends. She laments, "Don't call me Naomi. Call me Mara, because the Almighty has made my life very bitter. I went away full, but the LORD has brought me back empty. Why call me Naomi? The LORD has afflicted me; the Almighty has brought misfortune upon me" (Ruth 1:20-21). Naomi appears to be a bitter old woman who blames her God for her misfortunes rather than accepting personal responsibility. The truth is, her calamities were the result of her and her husband's choices.

But in Bethlehem Ruth will observe real godliness in street clothes.

**Godliness in Street Clothes**

I know a modern-day Boaz, except his name is Dave. Dave manages the Koinonia Conference Center south of Santa Cruz, California. I've never heard him preach a sermon or teach a Sunday school class. I don't even know if he holds any elected or appointed position in his church. He's never been to Bible school or seminary. What makes Dave so attractive is that he wears his godliness in street clothing.

When you wind up Eureka Canyon Road, framed by its giant eucalyptus trees, and turn into the conference center, you're impressed by how well everything is maintained. The grass is neatly trimmed, the buildings are well cared for, and the whole physical setting communicates peace. And one of the main reasons is because of Dave's leadership. He believes that our Lord is honored when we do our tasks with excellence.

I have been a speaker at the conference center for more than twenty years. (Isn't it amazing that they still haven't grown tired of me!) What impresses me is that every year some new feature is added or some convenience made available to serve those who come for renewal, encouragement or relaxation. Dave and his crew's creativity and dedication is evident everywhere.

When you meet Dave, you'll find him warm and gracious. He tends to stay in the background letting others do the up front activities. But if you get a chance to talk to him, you'll be impressed with his solid convictions, his deep love for what he does and his desire to serve those who come to the conference center. Because I've seen him over the years in many settings, I know that this man is the real thing.

Dave is strong in his manhood yet gracious and kind to women and children. He manifests a quiet strength that's winsome.

One of the greatest authorities on a man is his wife. Dave's wife, Kim, is quick to affirm the character and goodness she sees in him. In a recent conversation her face lit up as she said, "Dave is my Boaz. He's a gift from God!"

You might think that Dave has had an easy life. Actually he's had his share of adversities. But there is something godly inside Dave that's steadied his life like a ship's rudder. When others might have given up or tried to find answers in unhealthy or devious ways, he's kept his eye on the goal and continued to walk quietly with his Lord. I like Dave. I admire him. I respect him. He's a Boaz.

**Boaz: Godliness in Action**

We might wonder what Ruth was thinking and feeling that day when she walked down that dusty path to gather enough grain to provide a little nourishment for her and Naomi. We wonder if she might have been thinking something like this:

> *I hope they'll let me in this field. Some of these Israelites are mighty arrogant. Their prejudice against us Moabites oozes out of every pore in their body. What'll I do if they act hatefully because I'm an outsider? Will the women scorn me and act as though I'm not even here? What if some of the men make suggestive jokes about me or harass me sexually? Who would I turn to for protection?*

Whatever was going through her mind, Ruth was in for the surprise of her life. Today was her day to be introduced to a real man—a man of God.

When she got to the field that fateful day, she met Boaz. Like our friend Dave, he lived his godliness in street clothes. There was nothing "religious" about him, nothing phony. But there was a wealth of godliness. The biblical account gives us several characteristics of the Boaz brand of godliness.

*Godliness seen in eating and drinking with ordinary people.* When Boaz enters the field where his reapers are busy at work, there is no hint of aloofness or a condescending attitude toward those around him. People sense his warmth and friendliness to everyone. They know that he is the landowner but see him as a kind, caring person. When they see him coming down the road they smile, anticipating a friendly conversation with someone who cares for them.

Boaz noticed people. He inquired about them and observed them. He was able to discern their goodness of heart. He sat down and ate a meal with them rather than feeling the need to keep a social or professional distance. And we notice that his godliness is expressed in a most practical way: he served Ruth. He gave her abundant food with his own hands. How that must have touched her heart—an outcast woman warmly served by the landowner!

It's obvious that Ruth found this an unheard-of action. It is akin to the woman at the well's response to Jesus' kindness. "You are a Jew and I am a Samaritan woman. How can you ask me for a drink?" Jews and Samaritans didn't mingle. But Jesus, too, wore his godliness in street clothing. And it amazed people around him. In fact, one of the behaviors that irritated the religious establishment was that "this man welcomes sinners and eats with them" (Luke 15:2).

The Pharisees wore their "godliness" in elaborate robes and religious rituals. Jesus addresses them in this way: "Woe to you, teachers of the law and Pharisees, you hypocrites! You clean the outside of the cup and dish, but inside they are full of greed and self-indulgence. Blind Pharisee! First clean the inside of the cup and dish, and then the outside also will be clean" (Matthew 23:25-26). Later he described them as beautiful whitewashed tombs that are filled with dead men's bones and unclean things. "In the same way, on the outside you appear to people as righteous but on the inside you are full of hypocrisy and wickedness" (Matthew 23:28).

---

*"Every man has three characters—that which he exhibits, that which he has, and that which he thinks he has."*
***Alphonse Karr***

---

Earnest Christians can sometimes lose the honesty and transparency that accompanies true godliness. This happened to the apostle Peter after he had lived with Jesus and been commissioned to be a shepherd of God's people. In his letter to the Galatian Christians, Paul tells of his confrontation with Peter when Peter's fear of criticism caused him to treat Gentiles unkindly in the presence of Jews. Paul says to Peter, "You are a Jew, yet you live like a Gentile and not like a Jew. How is it, then, that you force Gentiles to follow Jewish customs?" (Galatians 2:14).

*Godliness revealed in words we speak.* Boaz is remarkable in his words. Notice his exquisite pattern of blessing others. He is consistently wishing others well, seeking the best for them. He desired that the blessing of God rest on them. In fact, the first words we hear from his mouth are his morning blessing on his employees.

Have you ever thought about how an employer treats his employees?

A Christian employer once asked me to help him build better staff morale within his company. Key individuals were planning to leave the company because they felt as though they were not valued and were not treated with respect. When I interviewed the employees, I found an interesting dynamic at work. Several workers said something like this: "Jack comes in the office, greets the receptionist, stops at two or three desks to chat with those workers and then goes into his office. Why doesn't he ever come to our desks to speak to us? He never shows any interest in us unless it's to critique our work." Other comments were "I work hard on my drafting, but all I'm told is what I'm doing wrong. What about all that I'm doing right? Doesn't that count?"

People like to know that they are valued.

This was a truth that Boaz believed and practiced. But even more significant, he expressed our Lord's love and value on them. He did this by blessing them on the Lord's behalf. Listen to his first meeting with Ruth. "May the LORD repay you for what you have done. May you be richly rewarded by the LORD, the God of Israel, under whose wings you have come to take refuge" (Ruth 2:12).

Do you hear what's happening? A destitute woman hears a man say, "I want my Lord to reward you richly. I want you to experience his abundant blessing on your life." How do you think this made Ruth feel? What a way to make her day! (And Boaz was eager to be a part of the Lord's blessing on this woman.)

Weeks later Ruth approaches Boaz as he lay sleeping where the grain was being threshed. When he awakes and finds Ruth there, he says, "The LORD bless you" to her. "I want my Lord to bring joy to your life." His constant pattern was his desire that his Lord's rich blessing fall on others.

What woman wouldn't be attracted to this lovely form of godliness? What woman wouldn't feel warmed and honored by a man who wanted our Lord's greatest treasures poured out on her? Some men are clever at flattering a woman to win points with her. Cunningly phrased words may be rooted in a desire to seduce others. But how much greater when the purity of heart is revealed, the desire that this individual rest in our Lord's blessing for that person's good, not for our gain.

*Godliness revealed in honoring commitments.* A country doctor received a phone call one rainy, blustery night. The caller said that his wife was ill and needed medical attention. "Will you come to our home to examine her?" the man asked.

The doctor, being a man of compassion, agreed to come, but made one request. "My car is disabled and in the repair shop," he said. "I'll need you to come and pick me so I can examine your wife."

The doctor was startled by the man's response. "What! In weather like this?" he replied.

While we may chuckle at the incident, it reminds us of the importance of commitment in relationships. We have observed Ruth and Naomi's desperate situation. They are dependent upon others who will have compassion and involve themselves in Ruth and Naomi's lives to bring support, encouragement and hope. Boaz proves to be an individual who expresses his godliness in practical terms. He involves himself in their lives in ways that will change their circumstances.

As the account of Ruth and Boaz unfolds, Naomi realizes that a more permanent solution to their dilemma must take place. So she envisions a plan whereby Ruth will seek Boaz's help. Ruth is counseled to ask Boaz to redeem her from her dire circumstances. He agrees, then verbalizes his commitment to see that she receives the help she and Naomi need. He says, "Stay here for the night, and in the morning if he [another man] wants to redeem, good; let him redeem. But if he is not willing, as surely as the LORD lives I will do it" (Ruth 3:13).

When Ruth returns home, she finds Naomi eager to know what had transpired. The mother-in-law quizzes her as to how the meeting with Boaz went. So Ruth relates the entire incident. When she's finished, Naomi replies, "The man will not rest until the matter is settled today" (Ruth 3:18). Naomi knows that Boaz is a man who can be counted on to keep his word. He will follow through on his commitments until the matter is resolved.

I've been emphasizing Boaz's practical godliness. Did you notice that his commitment is expressed with "as surely as the LORD lives I will do it." He is not hesitant to couch his commitments within the context of the Lord's reality to him. A woman cherishes a man who can be trusted to keep his word. Those who gain a reputation for following through on their word are admired.

*Godliness revealed in our view of others.* My friend Dave loves his wife. One way this is expressed is in his desire that her gifts and talents can be used to bless others. Kim has leadership skills that allow her to oversee the women's ministry of her church. Her dedication and gifting have resulted in a strong, vibrant ministry to many women. But without Dave's encouragement and support the task would have been very difficult.

I recall a time when Dave and Kim had picked Winnie and me up at the airport. During a leisurely seaside lunch and a ride to the conference center, the conversation turned to Kim's ministry to the women in their church. In a few well-chosen words Dave expressed his desire that Kim be able to utilize her gifts and bless others. It was clear that this man wanted what was best for his wife—even if he had to make personal sacrifices for it to occur.

When the apostle Paul gives counsel to husbands in his letter to the Ephesian Christians, he describes the effect of a husband's love on his wife. What makes the picture so powerful is that he couches it in a picture of how Christ's love impacts his bride, the church. He notes that such love beautifies the bride, bringing forth her glory, purifying her and increasing her loveliness (Ephesians 5:25-27).

Jesus Christ is committed to bring forth the loveliness of his bride. Boaz was committed to see the loveliness of Ruth shine forth. Godly men find joy in seeing women radiant, fulfilled and joyful. Women deeply appreciate men who are dedicated to their fulfillment.

*Godliness revealed in our desire for personal purity.* Boaz is an attractive man—attractive with the inner beauty of a pure heart and pure motives. He is an individual that is admired and respected by his employees. He is held in esteem by the townspeople. In every way he exemplifies a strong, successful, well-liked man. But one quality stands out as the mark of excellence in a man. That is his purity of heart.

In two incidents we see this man make clear his commitment to inner purity. In the first encounter with Ruth, Boaz tells her that he has instructed the men not to harass or abuse her. We can imagine him saying to the men, "You lay a hand on Ruth and you're history! If I hear of any inappropriate behavior toward her, you'll answer to me. Have you got that straight?"

But he also makes clear to Ruth that he has no intention of taking advantage of her. When she makes her nighttime visit to him at the threshing floor, it would have been easy for him to attempt to seduce her. But the biblical text makes it clear that his intention is to protect her reputation, not exploit her for his satisfaction. He sends her home before sunrise telling her, "No one must know that a woman was here at the threshing floor" (Ruth 3:14).

Our culture is saturated with sexual immorality, indecency and coarseness. It's not uncommon to hear men and women speak in vulgar and crude ways. Jesus said that our mouths speak from what has filled our hearts (Luke 6:45). Too often we hear communication that reveals ungodly thoughts and attitudes lodged in a sin-filled heart. By contrast there is a beauty and attractiveness in the man or woman who cultivates personal purity without being aloof, judgmental or prideful. Such pureness stands out like a light shining in the darkness.

*Godliness reveals how we use our resources.* Boaz is identified as a man of great wealth (Ruth 2:1). He owns land and has employees who work for him. He appears to be a person who is respected by Bethlehem's leaders. Life is good.

But we also note that Boaz demonstrates an unselfish spirit. His godliness reveals itself in an awareness that he is a steward of God's blessings. God had allowed him to prosper. But Boaz does not appear to hoard what he has or use it selfishly. Rather, he lives his life redemptively, making a difference in the lives of those around him. Because he was willing to expend his life for others, he left behind a legacy for generations to come.

I know of individuals who confess Jesus Christ as their sin bearer, but who live as self-centeredly as those who claim no relationship to him. They consume their resources on themselves with no concern for those around them. From all outward appearance they are investing little or nothing in what our Lord calls important. Biblical godliness is always linked with sharing our time, talents and material resources with those who are in need. James pulls no punches when he says, "Religion that God our Father accepts as pure and faultless is this: to look after orphans and widows in their distress and to keep oneself from being polluted by the world" (James 1:27).

**Godliness and Relationships**

I've said that there is a form of godliness that is merely an outward show without inner reality. Individuals can wear apparel that is associated with religious form but actually be ungodly toward our Lord and others. Jesus spoke of religious leaders in his day who were scrupulously "religious" in their outward form but who laid unreasonable burdens on others, cheated widows out of their homes and even denied their own parents of needed assistance.

In Boaz we observe a lovely, genuine godliness. It is godliness that attracts others and builds strong, vibrant relationships. In fact, as we observe Ruth, Boaz and the residents of Bethlehem, we can note several things that this "street clothes" godliness accomplishes.

First, we note that this kind of godliness makes a person attractive with an inner beauty. Peter noted that the godly beauty of a woman could be so powerful that it would win the heart of her husband, changing his behavior. He said that it was so significant that even our Lord found it a precious beauty (1 Peter 3:1-5). No doubt this was the godliness that Boaz saw in Ruth, the purity of heart that caused him to admire her so much. It glowed through her worn-out clothing for all to see.

Second, this kind of godliness reveals the heart of God. It demonstrates his heart of compassion and kindness. It discloses his desire to build up his people, not tear them down, to strengthen them and not sap their strength. It reveals our Lord as a joyous, celebrative God who enjoys being with those who seek him with a sincere heart.

---

*"I hope I shall possess firmness and virtue enough to maintain what I consider the most enviable of all titles, the character of an honest man."*
***George Washington***

---

Third, Boaz's kind of godliness unveils the character of our Lord. As his Spirit lives within us bringing about his transformation, we become people who are truthful, trustworthy, pure and unselfish. Jesus told Philip, "Anyone who has seen me has seen the Father" (John 14:9). When we have been with Jesus, others will see the beauty of his character fleshed out in us. They will see godliness in street clothes.

Fourth, Boaz's kind of godliness makes others want to know our Lord. Most of us can recount incidents we've witnessed or heard about professing Christians who have offended and wounded both Christians and non-Christians. The comment "If that's what it means to be a Christian, I don't want to be one" is painful to hear. Biblical godliness is remarkably attractive to those with tender, open hearts. No one could be godlier than Christ, and people flocked to him. People like Mary Magdalene found a beauty and grace in him that transformed her life.

Fifth, the godliness we see in Boaz gives people a sense of security in relationships. Biblical godliness makes us individuals who can be trusted. We become individuals who exhibit the character of our Lord, and others realize that they don't need to fear us.

While godliness is not a male virtue, Boaz makes a powerful case for the beauty that it creates in men. While both men and women are called to holiness of life, we believe that it is an especially attractive quality in men. We are saying that the man who wants to nurture healthy relationships with women—be it his wife, daughter or women in general—will want to concentrate on this aspect of his life. Just as godliness was one of those qualities that drew women to Jesus Christ, so it will foster those kinds of relationships between men and women and allow them to thrive.

**And Now the Rest of the Story**

A few days after the first draft of this chapter was finished, I was reading the Psalms. As I read, an inner light flashed on and an insight hit me. *There's Boaz!* Though I was reading about the Lord, I heard words that perfectly described what I'd read about this man of God. They were words that described practical godliness.

In Psalm 138:2 David writes, "I will give thanks to your name for your unfailing love and faithfulness because your promises are backed by all the honor of your name" (NLT). That's an apt description of Boaz. In the following verse David says, "You encourage me by giving me the strength I need." Those words could have come from Ruth's lips in describing Boaz!

In Psalm 146, David again speaks adoringly of our Lord, and we hear an echo of what we've seen in Ruth's rescuer.

- ☐ "He upholds the cause of the oppressed" (v. 7).
- ☐ "[He] gives food to the hungry" (v. 7).
- ☐ "He lifts up those who are bowed down" (v. 8).
- ☐ "The LORD watches over the alien" (v. 9).
- ☐ "[He] sustains the fatherless and the widow" (v. 9).

As the beauty of this truth washed over me, I was struck by the power of "godliness in street clothes." Boaz was revealing the heart of our Lord in his actions toward Ruth and Naomi. These women (and those who were watching on the sidelines) could observe God's passion acted out. It took away the starchiness of religious activity and portrayed righteousness that was attractive and winsome.

We are left with the engaging challenge to be like Boaz toward those around us. What an opportunity!

**What's Here for Us?**

1. Why do we more often associate godliness with women than with men?

2. What difference would it make to gender relationships if men ex-

hibited Boaz's "godliness in street clothes"?

3. We've often heard individuals say, "I'd rather deal with a non-Christian business person than a Christian." Do you agree or disagree with the statement? How could such a condition exist?

4. Who in your church do you think of when you think of godliness? What about them do you associate with godliness? Are the qualities "godliness in street clothes"?

5. Would people likely call you a godly person? Why or why not?

# 6

# Not the Brightest Bulb

A RECENT VISIT TO A WEB SITE REVEALED SOME HUMOROUS stories of folks who will be remembered for their lack of common sense.

☐ The crime column of a newspaper reported that a man walked into a fast-food restaurant early one morning. He waved a gun and demanded cash. The cashier explained that he couldn't open the cash register without a food order. The gunman ordered onion rings but was told that they weren't available for breakfast. Frustrated, the would-be robber turned and walked away.

☐ A man in Anniston, Alabama, was injured while attempting to replace a fuse in his pickup truck with a .22-caliber rifle bullet. (Apparently the bullet was a perfect fit.) Unfortunately when the electricity heated the bullet, it went off, shooting the man in the knee.

☐ John Smoltz, a pitcher for the Atlanta Braves, gave himself five-inch-long welts. The cause? He tried to iron his shirt—while wearing it. Smoltz defended himself by saying, "I've ironed that way five or six times and never had it happen."

☐ A man accused of drug possession appeared in court, claiming that he'd been searched without a warrant. The prosecutor explained that the officer didn't need a warrant because a "bulge" in the man's jacket could have been a gun. The defendant happened to be wearing the jacket that same day and handed it over so the judge could see it. "The judge discovered a packet of cocaine in the pocket and laughed so hard he required a five-minute recess to compose himself."

Like the judge, we can't help but laugh and shake our heads at the senseless things some people do. But relationships with those who lack wisdom are far from humorous. Proverbs 10:1 proclaims, "A wise son brings joy to his father, but a foolish son grief to his mother." And Proverbs 17:21 cautions, "To have a fool for a son brings grief; there is no joy for the father of a fool." Throughout the Bible God provides real examples of people who brought pain, suffering, ruin and heartache to themselves and others because of their foolishness. One man's wife said of him, "He is just like his name [Nabal]—his name is Fool, and folly goes with him" (1 Samuel 25:25). God also furnishes plenty of examples of those who were exalted, sought after and praised for their wisdom.

---

*"God discovers Himself to babes, and hides Himself in thick darkness from the wise and the prudent.*
*We must simplify our approach to Him.*
*We must strip down to essentials and they will be found to be blessedly few."*

***A. W. Tozer***

---

In any relationship wisdom is a cherished virtue—just check out Proverbs 4:7 in which Solomon urges, "Wisdom is supreme; therefore get wisdom." This is also a virtue that is evident in the character of Ruth. Her prudent decisions have positive long-term effects, and she welcomes the insight of others who have more experience than she does. Ruth's wisdom is part of her inner beauty—something that brings delight and warmth to those around her. Wisdom strengthens her relationships in powerful ways.

**The Woman of Wisdom**

Before we explore the importance of wisdom in relationships (particularly as it applies to women), it's interesting to note that modern society may not characterize women as wise. Past stereotypes have epitomized women as weak, helpless, dumb and thoughtless. (How many "dumb blonde" jokes have you heard? And they're always about women!) Although we've moved past many of those negative labels, there is still an undercurrent that may seep into our thinking. Women today are encouraged to be powerful, active, achievers, strong or "go-getters." But are they encouraged to be wise? Is prudence equaled with power? Women today may not even view wisdom as an attractive or desirable trait. (At first thought men may inwardly feel intimidated by a wise woman.) Most of us may never have considered the impact of wisdom on our relationships.

It's always interesting to turn from our point of view and take a look at God's perspective. (Using the Bible as a map, we often find that we're way off-track!) A quick perusal of the book of Proverbs reveals something intriguing: *Wisdom is always personified as female.*

"Wisdom calls aloud . . . she raises her voice in the public squares" (Proverbs 1:20).

"Blessed is the man who finds wisdom, the man who gains understanding, for she is more profitable than silver. . . . She is more precious than rubies" (Proverbs 3:13-14).

"Do not forsake wisdom, and she will protect you; love her, and she will watch over you. . . . Esteem her and she will exalt you; embrace her, and she will honor you" (Proverbs 4:6-8).

In addition, the Bible lifts up numerous examples of women who exemplify a sense of godly wisdom and insight. In fact, the models of wise women equal those of wise men! Consider Esther, the beautiful and prudent queen of Persia who saved the Israelites from genocide. Or Abigail, who displayed such amazing tact and humility that she swept David off his feet (1 Samuel 25). Then there was Priscilla, a companion and teacher of Paul and other men (Acts 18). The list of "wise women" could also include Lois and Eunice, the godly women who modeled their faith and passed it along to the apostle Timothy (2 Timothy 1:5). It's clear that wise men—such as Paul, Timothy and David—were drawn to insightful and prudent women. The same is true today—a discerning man will welcome a wise woman rather than be intimidated by her. Wisdom cultivates good, healthy relationships. God hasn't given us a catalog of dim or witless role models. He's filled his Word with vibrant examples of women who used godly wisdom to touch their world in powerful, meaningful ways. Ruth stands in good company, as an illustration of the power and influence of good judgment, discernment and godly wisdom.

---

*"The Scriptures do not make the mistake of confusing wisdom with other mental capacities or of giving wisdom less than its central place."*

***Lawrence O. Richards***

---

**Faith and Foresight**

Part of Ruth's wisdom is visible in the way she makes choices based on what *could* be rather than what *is*. In reading Ruth 1:1-9 we can't help but see the sadness and hopelessness of Ruth's situation. It might seem that Naomi is right—the best decision for Ruth *would* be to go back to Moab and join her family and friends there. Back home she might have more security, companionship and possibilities for a husband and family. But in Bethlehem what could Naomi possibly offer her? Ruth would be a stranger—possibly even an outcast! She would have to seek out work—maybe even hard physical labor! And certainly she would be lonely—perhaps she would never find a close friend!

But Ruth doesn't base her decision on her current circumstances. Rather, she seems to see beyond the here and now and look (with insight) at what will be or what could be. Perhaps Ruth believed that Naomi's family would provide for her. Maybe she saw the futility in the Moabite gods and wanted to seek the God of Naomi's people. Or it could be that Ruth simply liked Naomi and wanted to stick close to her mother-in-law. The Bible doesn't clearly spell out Ruth's reasons for staying with Naomi, but it *is* evident that she believed this was truly the best choice. She seemed to have a *spiritual perception* that guided her choices. For some reason Ruth believed that life with Naomi would be better than life back in Moab. Ruth's faith and foresight show the wisdom in her character.

Although our choices may be different, wisdom doesn't look much different today than it did for Ruth. In a "here-and-now" culture a wise person can be identified by his or her ability to forgo immediate results, with the understanding and foresight that another less obvious path will lead to things undeniably better. Godly wisdom partnered with patience can open doors to worlds we never imagined.

In his book *In the Eye of the Storm* Max Lucado gives a wonderful example of godly wisdom and foresight. He writes of a six-hour trip to Grandma's house for Thanksgiving in which his daughters get restless, hungry and impatient. Although the girls beg to stop for treats such as ice cream or pizza, Max and his wife are willing to wait for Grandma's succulent turkey and gravy. The long trip seems interminable to the young girls, but Max knows that the fun and fellowship that awaits them will be worth it. He closes with this view of God's wisdom, "Remember this: God may not do what you want, but he will do what is right . . . and best. He's the Father of forward motion. Trust him."[1]

Our circumstances may not be what we want—but they might be what God wants for us at the present. Wisdom means fixing our eyes on the prize rather than the difficulties around us. Wisdom means boldly trusting God and placing ourselves under his care. Wisdom means looking ahead and understanding that God has something magnificent planned for us—if we'll only wait.

**Seeking Wisdom**

Reading through the book of Ruth, you'll note that Ruth has great perception when it comes to people. She has a keen ability to choose trustworthy companions. Her partnership with Naomi leads to security, friendship and a reliable source of cultural information. Her decision to glean in Boaz's field is a wise one—it's a safe and friendly environment where a godly man conducts business. Perhaps one reason we're drawn to people of wisdom is that they maintain a standard of quality when it comes to friends. Please don't misinterpret this as saying that wise people are snobs! But understand that a sense of discernment will flow into every area of our lives—including our choice of companions. With good reason:

☐ "He who walks with the wise grows wise, but a companion of fools suffers harm" (Proverbs 13:20).
☐ "He who keeps the law is a discerning son, but a companion of gluttons disgraces his father" (Proverbs 28:7).
☐ "A man who loves wisdom brings joy to his father, but a companion of prostitutes squanders his wealth" (Proverbs 29:3).

Peers and associates have such enormous influence over our thinking, decision-making and worldview. Jody recalls an event that happened in her small community of Loveland, Colorado. She writes, "The headlines told of two teenage boys who broke into two local schools during spring break. The boys spent hours smashing computer screens, dumping out art supplies and using permanent markers to write on walls. The total damage was estimated at $30,000. In such a small community the teens were quickly caught. As it turned out, one of the boys had basically said, 'Hey, wouldn't it be fun to do this?' The other had simply come along for the ride." Because of this poor choice of friends, the second youth will spend several years in a juvenile detention center, separated from his family.

How often have you heard a similar story? A talented college athlete follows his friends in a prank and ends up permanently injured. A prosperous businessman fudges on his expense reports because "everyone does it." He is caught and loses his job. A young woman and her friends hang around with the wrong crowd—and she gets AIDS. The headlines (and our lives) are filled with stories of people who made a poor choice of friends and must reap heartbreaking consequences. A wise person is evidenced by his or her choice of quality friends, mentors and companions.

Not only does Ruth prudently choose her companions, she seeks (and listens to!) the wisdom they have to offer. Her "antennae" are tuned in to pick up what advice and guidance they have to offer. Boaz advises, "Don't go and glean in another field. . . . Stay here with my servant girls. Watch the field where the men are harvesting and follow along after the girls. I have told the men not to touch you. And whenever you are thirsty, go and get a drink from the water jars the men have filled" (Ruth 2:8-9). Ruth listens. It's obvious Boaz is watching out for Ruth's physical needs—safety, plentiful food and abundant water. Rather than tossing her head and saying, "No, I want to do things my way!" Ruth wisely accepts Boaz's offer.

Similarly, when Naomi counsels Ruth about the appropriate way to approach Boaz, Ruth welcomes Naomi's recommendations. She doesn't ignore the wise woman's words but follows them to the letter. Ruth is wise enough to listen to those who have much to teach her.

**Wisdom and Knowledge**

The beautiful thing about a wise person is that he or she is not afraid to seek counsel from others. In fact, someone with good judgment will *welcome* the knowledge of another! This brings up an important difference between knowledge and wisdom. When we speak of wisdom in this chapter, we're not referring to knowledge—at least the world's definition of knowledge. Although most of us would define knowledge as "smartness" or "intellectualism," the Bible equates knowledge with discernment or understanding, particularly as it applies to God and his ways.

"The fear of the LORD is the beginning of knowledge" (Proverbs 1:7).

"For God, who said, 'Let light shine out of darkness,' made his light shine in our hearts to give us the light of the knowledge of the glory of God in the face of Christ" (2 Corinthians 4:6).

"We have not stopped praying for you and asking God to fill you with the knowledge of his will through all spiritual wisdom and understanding" (Colossians 1:9).

"But grow in the grace and knowledge of our Lord and Savior Jesus Christ" (2 Peter 3:18).

---

*"I am an omnivorous reader, with an extremely retentive memory for trifles."*
***Sherlock Holmes***

---

Rather than extolling "smartness," we want to lift up the attractiveness of good judgment or *discernment.* When in doubt, a foolish person might trust his or her own knowledge, even if it is lacking or shortsighted. On the other hand a wise person isn't afraid to rely on the knowledge of another. This is just one more way that wisdom has a powerful impact on our relationships.

"My husband Erik awoke one night with terrible stomach pain," writes Jody. "We were unsure of the cause—it could have been the stomach flu, a torn muscle, a hernia or even his appendix. Consulting a medical handbook only confused us further, since there were so many things that listed 'abdominal pain' as a symptom. After praying for wisdom, we finally called the doctor, who advised us to get to the emergency room because the cause was most likely appendicitis. A few hours later I was face to face with a surgeon who had just removed a terribly infected appendix—one that would have burst if we hadn't been urged to get to the hospital."

---

*"Wisdom is meaningless until our own experience has given it meaning . . . and there is wisdom in the selection of wisdom."*
***Bergen Evans***

---

Had Jody and Erik relied on their own *knowledge*, Erik's condition could have drastically worsened and become serious—even deadly! Instead, they sought God's *wisdom* and the competent knowledge of a doctor. The appendix was removed, and health was restored.

God doesn't expect you to know everything! (Isn't that a relief?) That's why he lovingly surrounds us with people who have a variety of wonderful skills, talents, insights and abilities. The man or woman who displays godly wisdom will access those people—that source of knowledge—rather than guessing or pretending to have all the answers. Remember, seeking the knowledge of others is not a sign of weakness or inability. Rather, it is a clear sign of insight and wisdom.

---

*"Knowledge is horizontal. Wisdom is vertical—*
*it comes down from above."*
***Billy Graham***

---

**Moral Foolishness**

Few people today would admit to being a fool. Instead, we've incorporated new words that sound a little more, well, exciting. We describe people as "reckless," "a little silly" or "extreme." Sometimes we try to put a positive spin on the characteristic by saying, "She's just really headstrong," or "He likes to make his own decisions." But at the heart of the matter these are foolish persons. Just as we are drawn to people who display godly wisdom, those who are foolish (often subconsciously) repel us. We may shake our heads and chuckle at the antics, but there is no appeal or desire to get closer. You can be certain that a foolish heart or attitude has a damaging effect on a relationship.

As we explore the effect of foolishness on a relationship, it's interesting to note that there are three Hebrew words used for "fool," "foolish" or "folly." All three terms view foolishness as a moral—rather than an intellectual—issue.[2] These moral deficiencies lead to tremendous heartache and grief in any relationship.

The first term represents the person who is insolent or rebellious, and is revealed by a quick temper. James 1:19 encourages us, "My dear brothers, take note of this: Everyone should be quick to listen, slow to speak and slow to become angry, for man's anger does not bring out the righteous life that God desires." What *does* a quick temper or insolence bring about? Think of a time when you've lost your temper. What happened? Maybe you said a few choice words when the lawnmower wouldn't work. (The lawnmower didn't mind, but your neighbors certainly got an earful!) Or you lost it when your child talked back to you, so you threw the nearest object in his or her direction. (Now you have a broken lamp *and* a damaged relationship to go along with it.) Perhaps you were irritated at a coworker and said some hasty, unkind words. (Unfortunately those are impossible to take back.)

*"[Wisdom] involves the knowledge of God and of the intricacies of the human heart."*
***J. Oswald Sanders***

Any way you look at it, insolence or quick-tempered actions bring negative results to our relationships. Fear, mistrust and loss of respect are just a few of the effects that such a fool will leave in his or her wake. According to Proverbs 22:15, this fool is childish, and pain is just about the only thing that will cause him or her to wake up and smell the coffee. Unfortunately all too often a dear friend, coworker or family member is the first to feel that pain.

The second type of fool is the one who is stubborn, making poor choices that only lead to destruction. King Saul is just one example Scripture offers of such a fool. He repeatedly disregarded Samuel's (and the Lord's) instructions, he persisted in hunting David, and he tried to take matters into his own hands by consulting a witch. In response to Saul's actions God tells Samuel, "I am grieved that I have made Saul king, because he has turned away from me and has not carried out my instructions" (1 Samuel 15:11). Saul's choices lead to his demise and the pain and suffering of his family.

Such stubborn foolishness grieves God today and mars our relationships with pain and frustration. Consider the husband who won't accept counsel about his drinking habits. "I can lick this on my own," he says. Think of the daughter who slips out of the house late at night. "My parents don't know what they're talking about," she mutters. Ponder the young man who refuses premarital counseling. "Those people, what do they know?" he argues. Pride obscures wisdom. Obstinate spirits march forward, trampling over the hearts of those they love most.

The third Hebrew term for "fool" refers to one's inner disposition. This fool turns completely away from God and closes the door. Immorality and outright defiance of God's commands mark his or her life like graffiti on a wall. Genesis gives us the picture of such a fool in Abraham's nephew Lot, a greedy fool who settles in a wicked city. Although Lot is "righteous," he unwisely surrounds himself and his family members with incredible depravity. When God warns Lot that the city is to be destroyed, Lot exhorts his future sons-in-law to leave. But they think he's joking! To his family Lot has lost all moral integrity. Not only does Lot offer his virgin daughters to be raped by a vile crowd, but he then hesitates to leave such a sinful city! Lot's immorality carries on to his daughters, who bear his children—who become the Moabites and Ammonites. These tribes became bitter enemies of Abraham's descendants. Such grievous sin eventually brought death and unbearable suffering to many.

Although it's easy to look at Lot and feel superior, it's crucial that we remember this truth: without a fear of the Lord we are all fools who despise wisdom. "The fear of the LORD is the beginning of knowledge, but fools despise wisdom and discipline" (Proverbs 1:7). Have you ever seen a married couple in which one person is a fervent Christian and the other doesn't have a relationship with Christ? How would you describe that relationship? What emotions does the Christian feel every day? It's a painful and discouraging thing to be a part of such a relationship. A deep, loving relationship with one who doesn't profess to know Christ will inevitably bring heartache—on a daily basis.

Many of us have been burned in relationships with foolish people. Their insensitive comments hurt. Their thoughtless actions leave us lonely. And with every careless word or deed we step a little farther away, if only to avoid the pain. Emotional and relational isolation, grief, mistrust, loss of respect or integrity, these are just a few effects of foolishness. When we explore the painful results of foolishness, it makes sense that we seek relationships with those who are wise.

**The Proverbs 31 Woman**

One of God's greatest examples of wisdom is spelled out in the actions and characteristics of a woman. The "Proverbs 31 Woman," as she is often called, is the epitome of a prudent woman. Through her, God has given us a clear picture of wisdom.

"Her husband has full confidence in her" (Proverbs 31:11).

*He trusts her judgment and knows that she won't make foolish decisions.*

"She considers a field and buys it" (Proverbs 31:16). *She uses discretion, rather than hastily choosing.*

"She sees that her trading is profitable" (Proverbs 31:18). *This woman uses wisdom in all business dealings, seeking what is best.*

"She speaks with wisdom, and faithful instruction is on her tongue" (Proverbs 31:26). *A virtuous woman uses thoughtful words rather than blurting something out without thinking. She pursues wisdom, not popularity.*

"Her children arise and call her blessed; her husband also, and he praises her" (Proverbs 31:28). *This woman's home is harmonious—love is spoken openly, affirmations abound.*

As you read this passage, be sure you don't miss something vital. How does this woman's wisdom impact her relationships? Her husband trusts her, praises her and is even respected himself. Her children praise her and have faith in her. This "noble" woman has secure, healthy relationships! Wisdom can have the same impact on our relationships today—cultivating trust, affirmation, security and peace.

**Lucy . . . What Have You Done Now?**

As comical as it was, the old television show *I Love Lucy* gives us an excellent example of what happens to a relationship when foolishness is involved. Lucy's silly antics lead Ricky to become suspicious of her and often set up rivalry between the two. Obviously the writers of the show created some hilarious scenarios from this lack of trust—it made for some wonderfully delightful episodes! But in everyday life we crave trust and security in our relationships. We want to be around people who have faith in us and whom we can rely on. We find peace when we're around trustworthy people.

Wisdom brings a sense of trust to a relationship. When you are characterized by prudence, I don't have to doubt your every move. When I continually display insight, you don't need to worry about me. Think about the relationship between a parent and toddler. The toddler is not wise—he or she is just learning about the world and how things work. Therefore, the parent must constantly watch and consistently check in. Even when things are quiet (or should I say, *especially* when things are quiet?), there is a tension. The parent is always "on guard." This is normal and healthy for a parent-toddler relationship—but can you imagine it in an adult relationship? (Yes, unfortunately there are some adult "toddlers"!) Rather than the unease of mistrust, thriving relationships will display a peace that comes from trust.

---

*"The first point of wisdom is to discern that which is false, the second, to know that which is true."*
***Lantantius***

---

Jody and her sister Amy often watch each other's children. Because Jody knows that Amy is a woman of prudence and discernment, she can trust Amy. So when Jody leaves little Brianna with Aunt Amy, Jody can go away with complete peace and trust. She doesn't need to constantly check in. She doesn't need to worry that things will get out of control. She doesn't need to spend time wondering if she's done the right thing. Because there is a bond of trust, peace flows through the relationship. It is clearly a firm friendship to all who witness it.

Because we are drawn to people who display wisdom, those relationships will carry a sense of respect or admiration. Remember, the husband and children of the Proverbs 31 woman praised her. As we watch a prudent person make good choices, we affirm those choices. And as we affirm, our relationship is deepened. Love and friendship grow. The relationship becomes something warm and positive. (No wonder we seek such relationships!)

Mutual respect and admiration can be displayed in so many ways—an encouraging note, a hug, a simple "I'm proud of you" or added responsibility. In a work relationship such affirmations bolster teamwork and lead to increased job satisfaction (which can lead to increased productivity). In a friendship these encouraging acts deepen the relationship and allow it to grow in new ways. In a marriage affirming words strengthen and renew love. Honoring another for his or her wisdom will only make a relationship stronger.

In this chapter we've explored how foolishness leads to relationships plagued by problems. In the same way wisdom leads to relationships unmarred by problems. *This is not to say that wise people don't have problems!* But those who display godly insight and discernment can better navigate the same difficulties that the fool will needlessly encounter. Because of this, prudence breeds a sense of security in relationships. Foolish disputes don't have to happen. Pointless problems may never arise. Senseless pitfalls can be sidestepped. The relationship is secure—a haven from many unnecessary problems. And when life's difficulties do come along, wise individuals have the tools to effectively manage conflict.

**Get Wisdom!**

The book of Proverbs continually exhorts us to "get wisdom." The effects are long-lasting, life changing and bring incredible peace to our relationships. Ruth's use of godly discernment changed her life in countless ways. She went from a penniless foreigner to the wife of an influential businessman. No longer a widow, Ruth became a wife. Her faith grew. Her family grew. And God brought about his plan in amazing ways. He can do the same with you.

**What's Here for Us?**

1. Who are some people you would consider wise? Why do you consider them to be wise?
2. How have these wise people positively influenced your life?
3. In which areas of your life do you most need wisdom? How can you follow the words in Proverbs and "get wisdom"?
4. Think of one specific way you can cultivate wisdom today.

# 7

# Gentlemen Versus Gentle Men

IF YOU LOOK UP THE WORD *GENTLEMAN* IN YOUR DICTIONARY, you'll find definitions similar to these:

☐ a man of noble or gentle birth

☐ a man who is of the landed gentry

☐ a man who combines a gentle birth or rank with chivalrous qualities

☐ a man whose conduct conforms to a high standard of propriety or correct behavior

☐ a man of independent means who does not engage in any occupation or profession for gain

☐ a man who does not engage in menial occupation or in manual labor for gain

☐ a man of any social class or condition[1]

Did you notice that of the many definitions, none mentions

that the man would be characterized as gentle? A man could be considered a gentleman and never be gentle. That seems odd.

Today it's rare to hear someone describe a man as a gentleman. Although it was more common in years past, usually the speaker was referring to a man who distinguished himself with certain commendable character traits. You knew that a gentleman would treat women and children with courtesy and kindness. You could count on a gentleman to rescue them if they were in danger or threatened with abuse. A gentleman was an individual who embraced virtues that women and children admired. It made the gentleman attractive in their eyes. Someone to look up to. Someone to appreciate.

*Gentle* men are special men. King James I said, "I can make a lord, but only the Almighty can make a gentleman."[2] William Makepeace Thackery said, "Perhaps a gentleman is a rarer man than some of us think. Which of us can point out many such in his circle; men whose aims are generous, whose truth is not only constant in its kind, but elevated in its degree; whose want of meanness makes them simple, who can look the world honestly in the face with an equal manly sympathy for the great and the small?"[3]

---

*"The Scripture speaks of no real Christian who has an ugly, selfish, angry, and contentious spirit. Nothing can be more contradictory than a morose, hard, closed, and spiteful Christian."*
***Gary Thomas***

---

Boaz was of this lineage. He was one whom our Lord had shaped into a *gentle*-man. But he was not only a gentleman in godly stature and manner, he was also a gentle *man,* who related to Ruth and Naomi in the spirit of that soft touch that refreshed their impoverished spirits. Proverbs 15:4 reminds us that "gentle words bring life and health" (NLT). This remarkable man's words and actions renewed the two destitute women's hope in humanity and suggested the possibility of a bright future.

**The World of Brawn**

Through the centuries most heroes and villains have distinguished themselves for their physical strength and prowess. Many seem to be attracted to the Rambo image of brawn, blood and guts. If the person carries an AK-47 and blows away anyone who gets in his path, he becomes our hero. Too often our children are fed this diet with tragic results.

Inhumanities that make our skin crawl have been recorded in every period of history. As we write this book, we are hearing daily of men who are raping, killing and pillaging people of another ethnic background. These killers are mean, harsh and cruel. They have no compassion for those they are driving from their homes. They care nothing for the children that are left as homeless orphans.

In an earlier chapter I mentioned Nabal, a contemporary of David, who was known by all as one who was mean and surly in all his relationships. One of his own servants described him as "such a wicked man that no one can talk to him" (1 Samuel 25:17). He could care less that someone at his doorstep was hungry, and he had an abundance of food to feed him or her.

In the Old Testament book of Esther we're told of an evil man named Haman, who had worked his way to a place of great influence with King Xerxes. Because Haman had nursed a hatred for the Jews, he used his power to manipulate the king to sign a decree that would mean the death of all Jews. Only the intervention of a sovereign God kept this wicked man from using his corrupted power to destroy innocent people.

---

*"If we want to demonstrate the uncommon grace of Jesus to a world that worships power, we must set aside our combativeness to embrace gentleness."*
***John Vawter***

---

Even in Ruth's day there were men who could not be trusted to act honorably toward women. Boaz makes it clear that he thinks some of his employees are not above using Ruth to satisfy their lust. Certainly these are not *gentle* men. Some men would never stoop to the attitudes of Nabal, but they've adopted a "don't expect me to be gentle" attitude toward those they profess to love. I was reminded of this while reading the account of a man I'll fictitiously call "Sam." Sam believed that only sissies showed courtesy toward women. So he never opened a door for his wife. He'd make remarks like "She doesn't have broken arms. She can open it herself."

After many years of marriage Sam's wife died, and he found how much he missed her. For the first time he experienced overwhelming grief. He realized how much he loved her.

At her funeral as the pallbearers carried her casket to the hearse where Sam stood, the mortician knew him well and called out to Sam, "Open the door for her, will you?" As Sam reached for the door handle, he froze. At that instant the thought flashed through his mind, *I never opened a door for her in life; now in her death this is my last and only time.* The regret for his insensitive and callused spirit rushed upon him, and he wept.

### The Incredible Power of Gentleness

In the New Testament the Greek word *praus* is usually translated "meek" or "gentle." It was a word that was used to describe a stallion that had been trained to be gentle. Prior to discipline wild, fierce energy allowed the creature to run wild and do as he pleased. But training brought a new dimension to this magnificent stallion. He retained all his power—his muscles could ripple with strength—but he was meek and peaceful. A child could be placed on his saddle, and he would carry her with gentleness. *That's an impressive word picture!*

---

*"Gentle living is blessed living. It's soothing, refreshing, bathing people in the presence of Christ."*
**Gary Thomas**

---

**The Context for Gentleness**

Let's think for a few minutes about power in relationships. After all, gentleness only becomes significant in the context of power and strength. First, *all of us have some kind of relational power.* Even infants have power. (Power to get a sleepy-eyed mom or dad up in the middle of the night!) Young children quickly learn how to manipulate their parents to get what they want. That's power. A young woman learns how to use her assets to get her boyfriend to do what she wants. That's power.

Second, *it's not wrong to have power.* The issue is how we use that power. Do we use it for selfish ends? Or do we use it for genuine good? All of us have some kind of power. We need to ask, "How am I using the power that has been entrusted to me?"

---

*"The measure of a man is what he does with power."*
**Pittacus**

---

Third, *power may be expressed knowingly or unknowingly.* Often an individual thinks he or she is powerless but the perceptive observer will see clear indications of subtle power in action. For example, Sheila is married to Tom, a domineering husband. He bosses her around and exerts control in many areas of her life. But if you watch Sheila closely, you'll notice that she gets her licks in, too. She is incredibly clever at undermining Tom's self-esteem and heightening his feelings of guilt. She lets him know that she sees him as a failure, and it hurts him deeply.

You'd better believe that she's yielding power over her domineering husband. But while Tom is open and obvious in his display, Sheila is subtle and sneaky.

**What Power Do I Have?**

All of us have power in some form. You might ask, "How is power exhibited?" It's important to recognize the various manifestations of power so we can spot its presence in our own relationships.

Power is wielded *through our personalities*. We've heard someone describe a person as "an overpowering personality." She might have charisma that moves another person's emotions and actions. Or power may be expressed through a domineering personality. Some people are forceful, insistent or controlling.

Power exists *through position*. It could be family position—"I'm your dad and you'll do as I say"; business position—"Since he owns the company, he gets to call the shots"; social position—"I wouldn't consider dating him. It would be beneath me"; or assigned position—"When I see a police car following me, I feel the hair on my neck rise."

While writing this chapter I was reminded of an incident that occurred while I was in graduate studies. I took a class in group dynamics at a local university. On the first day of class the professor said, "We'll conduct this class like a group of equals. Treat me as one of your peers." But I found I had an emotional barrier against this. I'd been taught all my life that someone who had an earned doctorate should be addressed as "Doctor." The power of position had been thoroughly ingrained in my brain, and it refused to be rooted out.

Power is also granted *to the expert.* When we go to a medical doctor, we grant him power to poke, prod and penetrate our body because he's the "expert," and we assume he knows what's wrong with us. Then he gives us a piece of paper with illegible writing that we take to the pharmacist. "Take two of these red pills four times a day," we're told. And we do as we're told because "she's the expert."

Then too, *those who have resources* have power. Resources such as money, property or time. When we are dependent on another's resources, that person has power over us.

A graduate student was describing his relationship with his bride of six months. He said that the major problem they'd encountered was who would control the spending of their money. Because his wife was the primary wage earner, she assumed that she should have more power in determining where it would be spent.

The student said, "I was aware of the problem long before my wife was. So I took the challenge and learned all I could about money management. I determined to demonstrate to her that I was competent to make wise financial decisions. The outcome was that we decided to compromise where we shared the control of our finances. Now we're both happier with shared power."

We've not intended to make an exhaustive list of sources of power. The point is that we all have power to bless or curse others. It is not wrong to have this power—sometimes it has been entrusted to us directly by our Lord. But we are responsible to be godly stewards of this trust. We can use the designated power to selfishly lord it over others and get what we want, or we can exercise it gently to bless them.

**Biblical Models of Gentleness**

Boaz had power. He had the power of wealth. He had power over his employees to make their lives joyful or miserable. He had power over Ruth. He could have denied her access to his field. Or he could have let her pick up leftovers and instructed his employees to leave nothing but scraps behind. Boaz had the power of social position in his community. He was influential and could use that to enrich other's lives or use it for selfish gain.

As we read the account of Ruth and Boaz, it is apparent that this compassionate man chose to use his power to bless Ruth. And he asserted the power with gentleness so that she didn't have to fear him or resent his "lording it over her." Such actions never happened. Rather he used his position, his resources and his personality to bless her beyond her fondest imagination.

**Window 1: Jesus Christ**

In examining the Bible we've discovered three significant windows through which we can view the meek or gentle person. The clearest and most compelling is seen in Jesus Christ. Through his words and actions it is apparent that he is the model *par excellence* of gentleness. Jesus is *the* gentleman.

---

*"Though our Saviour's passion is over,*
*his compassion is not."*
***William Penn***

---

Individuals in every age since Christ walked on earth have found hope and encouragement in his words, "Come to me, all you who are weary and burdened, and I will give you rest. Take my yoke upon you and learn from me, for I am gentle and humble in heart, and you will find rest for your souls" (Matthew 11:28-29).

These words take on even greater power as we watch our Lord kneeling before his disciples with towel and washbowl. With tenderness he lovingly washes each man's feet and wipes away the water. Peter found this act so humbling that initially he refused to allow his Lord to do such a lowly task. But Jesus insisted that Peter allow the Son of God to minister to him in this tender act.

Charles Rann Kennedy wrote the play *The Terrible Meek.* In a scene at the cross a centurion talks with Mary. He says, "I tell you, woman, that this dead Son of yours, disfigured, shamed, spat upon, has built this day a kingdom that can never die. The living glory of him rules it. The earth is his and he made it. He and his brothers have been molding and making it through the long ages; they are the only ones who ever did possess it; not the proud, not the idle, not the vaunting empires of the world. Something has happened on this earth today to shake all the kingdoms of blood and fear to dust. The earth is his, the earth is theirs and they made it. The meek, the terrible meek, the fierce agonizing meek are about to enter into their inheritance."[4]

**Window 2: Gentle Women**

As the apostle Peter wrote to his beloved flock, he gave a personal challenge to wives concerning their relationship with their husbands. In it he makes a profound statement. Peter says that a wife's submissive attitude toward her husband could so powerfully impact him that he comes to believe God's truth.

The wife's behavior would convince her husband that the Word of God was relevant to his own life. (How's that for power?)

---

*"Power in the Christian life depends upon our connection with the source of power."*
***L. Nelson Bell***

---

But Peter isn't finished. He continues his counsel, challenging women to put a priority on developing their inner beauty rather than merely outer beauty. Listen to the wise apostle's counsel. "Instead, it should be that of your inner self, the unfading beauty of a gentle and quiet spirit, which is of great worth in God's sight" (1 Peter 3:4). He reminds women that a gentle spirit is an unfading beauty that even touches our Lord's heart. Imagine that! Our Lord gazing at you with a wondering eye and a joyous heart as he sees within you this quiet and gentle spirit.

**Window 3: Gentle Leaders**

We discovered another group of people that Paul selected to challenge to gentleness—godly leaders. In fact, he identifies gentleness as a personal quality that he nurtured in his relationship with the Thessalonian Christians. Paul affirms this as one of the important qualities that caused them to take his message seriously. It affirmed that he was for real.

As he talks about this, he contrasts the power of gentleness with the power of position. Paul says, "As apostles of Christ we could have been a burden to you, but we were gentle among you, like a mother caring for her little children" (1 Thessalonians 2:6-7). Do you see what Paul is saying? He had the valid authority to come emphasizing his apostolic authority ("I'm an apostle of the living God. Listen to me"). But he recognized the greater power of gentleness, because *gentle-*

*ness penetrates the heart more powerfully than position.*

---

*"The real function of power and the order it creates is the liberation of men and women to think and be and make the most of themselves."*
***Adolf Berle***

---

Beyond his own example Paul also directly challenges leaders to excel in gentleness. He instructs his protégé Timothy concerning how spiritual shepherds relate to their sheep. He says that "those who oppose him he must gently instruct, in the hope that God will grant them repentance leading them to a knowledge of the truth" (2 Timothy 2:25). When he writes to the Galatian leaders, he reminds them that they are to restore wayward individuals in a spirit of gentleness and humility (Galatians 6:1).

**Leaders Must Lead in Gentleness**

Jody works for a Christian organization that endeavors to apply biblical principles in relationships among employees. The company structure is laid out in an upside-down triangle, with the CEO and founder of the company at the bottom. Supervisors will tell you, "I *serve* a team of individuals" rather than "I'm the boss of a group of people." This humble, servant attitude pervades everything in the company—leaders genuinely seek to gently serve others, regardless of position or status. Jody can tell you, it's a delightful environment in which to work, because godliness and gentleness is modeled in every leader.

**Gentleness's Mighty Power**

What makes such a seemingly "soft" quality so powerful? Why the big emphasis on gentleness? Is it really that important? Well, consider the following four effects gentleness has on relationships.

*When we lead with gentleness, others don't fear our strength.* We've emphasized that godly men will clothe themselves with gentleness. Men are often placed in positions of leadership. They will encounter people who have been run over by individuals who use the power of their position to beat up on people. So when these people meet a gentle leader, their anger or fear will be defused, and they will respond to the leader more positively. This principle applies whether you're called to lead in your home, place of work, church or community.

---

*"I often say of George Washington that he was one of the few in the whole history of the world who was not carried away by power."*
***Robert Frost***

---

*Gentleness nurtures trust and confidence.* When Boaz approaches Ruth with gentleness and kindness, she is overwhelmed with gratitude. Her response is, "You have given me comfort and have spoken kindly to your servant—though I do not have the standing of one of your servant girls" (Ruth 2:13). Boaz's actions caught her off guard, and she received something she never expected. He spoke to her heart and laid the foundation whereby she can begin to trust him.

In the 1970s David Aikman was assigned to Southeast Asia as a correspondent for *Time* magazine. He had come to faith in Jesus Christ and devoted himself to follow his leadership. As the Spirit of God drew him closer to his Lord, David began to wonder if the Lord wanted him in some form of pastoral or mission ministry. A ministry opportunity opened to him that seemed like a dream come true.

David sought God's wisdom in prayer and through godly counsel. Most people encouraged him to pursue this attractive opportunity. As the moment of decision approached, he attended a twelve-man prayer breakfast at a luxury hotel in Hong Kong. There he laid the matter before these godly men.

Following the meeting, a soft-spoken Southern Baptist missionary approached Aikman. David describes the encounter in this way:

> He was kind and meek, and almost never volunteered his opinion on things. I thought that he might want to talk about his work with Chinese young people in Hong Kong.
>
> But it wasn't that at all. "David," he said gently, as if he doubted he had the right to speak to me at all about it, "I've been thinking about your prayer request. I just wonder if you aren't right now in exactly the place that God wants you to be."
>
> The impact upon me could not have been greater if fire had come down from the ceiling and burned his words into the expensive silk wallpaper. I knew the Lord was speaking directly through him. The Holy Spirit took the man's barely audible, hesitantly articulated "thought" and turned it into a thundering piece of heavenly guidance. I grasped perfectly that I wasn't, for the foreseeable future, supposed to make any job move.[5]

*Gentleness opens the door for protection.* Jesus' invitation in Matthew 11:18-30 provides us with a resting place when weary, if we believe that he is gentle and humble in heart. We'll come into the shelter of his protective care, if we don't have to fear his wrath. In like manner others will allow us to protect them if they are not afraid of us.

---

*"Power corrupts the few,*
*while weakness corrupts the many."*
***Eric Hoffer***

---

By contrast, we think of a young woman we'll call Shelley,

who longed for her dad's protection, but because he was so harsh and demanding, she became fearful to approach him. Though she longed for protection, she never dared come to him. His critical spirit was too painful to endure.

*Gentleness creates the context for bonding to occur.* We've said before that gentleness is one of those rare qualities that touch another person's heart. When accompanied with an unconditional love, others can't help but be drawn to us. It's the same irresistible power that draws us to our heavenly Father's heart. David said, "How priceless is your unfailing love!" (Psalm 36:7). This love always comes in gentleness. Even as our Lord delights to see it in his children, so we are captured by its beauty and warmth when we experience it in others.

*Gentleness defuses anger and hostility.* The writer of the Proverbs reminds us that "A gentle answer turns away wrath, but a harsh word stirs up anger" (Proverbs 15:1). This principle has been tested time and again. We live in a world that bombards us with issues, problems and pressures. The stress level soars. But when we encounter the quiet and gentle person, it's like coming into the presence of Jesus. "Come and rest."

**What's Here for Us?**

1. Describe two gentle men you know who fit the description we've given in this chapter.

2. What makes a gentle person strong?

3. What difference does it make to you that Jesus and the apostle Paul described themselves as gentle?

4. Do you agree or disagree with the following statement: "It's more important for men to be gentle than for women"? Explain your answer.

5. What difference would it make in your church if *all* men were gentle?

6. Identify a person you know who is gentle. How has that shaped your relationship with him or her?

7. Would people likely describe you as gentle? If not, how would they describe you?

8. Which people in your circle of relationships need a gentle person to encourage or befriend them?

9. What in this chapter challenges you personally to become more gentle in your relationships?

# 8

# A Firm Resolve—A Steadfast Heart

YOUNG TOM HAD MANY REASONS TO BE DISCOURAGED. AS A child he'd had only three short months of formal education—and even then his schoolmaster considered him to be retarded.[1] If that weren't bad enough, his hearing was seriously impaired. A tinkerer, Tom's earliest innovations failed. But his determination couldn't be doused by such setbacks. Tom kept inventing, designing and drafting, looking for ways to improve and ease the quality of life. Thomas Edison, the boy once considered retarded, would eventually "tinker" his way to over one thousand patents for useful inventions such as the phonograph and the light bulb. Today he is widely regarded as the greatest inventive genius who ever lived.

Joe had a rough start too. While he was still a teenager, he was alienated from his family and almost left to die. He soon found himself penniless, working as a lowly servant in the home of a wealthy man. If that wasn't bad enough, Joe was accused of attempted rape and sent to prison. Things truly looked grim. But Joe didn't give up. The prison guards noted Joe's persistence and hard work and gradually gave him more and more responsibility. Within a few years Joe was second in command for the most powerful man in the country. Joe's determination brought him from the depths of an empty well, to a powerful position in Egypt. The book of Genesis clearly shows that God used "Joe" to save thousands of lives and restore Jacob's broken family relationships.

Whether we find them in the newspapers, history books or in the Bible, such stories of distinguished men or women inspire us to perseverance. When we hear of athletes who overcome daunting challenges, students who put in incredible hours of studying or celebrities who rise above harsh circumstances, we marvel at their determination—the firm resolve that pushed them to succeed. We often look at these people as heroes who bravely conquered a foe such as poverty, handicap, hatred or discouragement. There is an intangible beauty evident in a determined spirit. It attracts us, inspires us and moves us.

---

*"History is the record of an encounter between character and circumstance."*
***Donald Creighton***

---

Ruth's determination was a key to her success in life and in her relationships. When life looked grim and circumstances seemed hopeless, Ruth didn't quit. When those around her gave up and turned away, Ruth set her eyes on God and moved forward. When it would have been easier to turn around and head for home, Ruth took the challenging path that would draw her closer to God and to others. We can learn much from this woman who dug in her heels and resolved that tragedy wouldn't be the victor. Her persistence led Ruth to a new home, gave her an extended family, opened the doors to a prominent social position and drew her to the man who would provide for and love her.

### A Tenacious Woman

Ruth's tenacity is evident from the moment we're introduced to her. Her first words are ones of commitment and loyalty as she and her sister-in-law declare to Naomi, "We will go back with you to your people" (Ruth 1:10). Certainly it would have been easier to go back to Moab, where she likely had friends and family to comfort her. But Ruth is committed to Naomi. Her heart is drawn to the heart of this older woman. After Orpah turns tail and heads for Moab, Ruth again proclaims this covenant to Naomi, "Don't urge me to leave you or to turn back from you. Where you go I will go, and where you stay I will stay. Your people will be my people and your God my God. Where you die I will die, and there I will be buried. May the LORD deal with me, be it ever so severely, if anything but death separates you and me" (Ruth 1:16-17). Note that Ruth doesn't whine and beg Naomi. She doesn't cajole or whimper. She is deliberate and specific in her intentions. She speaks them with clarity and firmness. Her words are a clear signal to Naomi that she means business. From this point on Ruth is characterized by persistence. In Bethlehem her commitment to hard work shows she's not a quitter. As Ruth labors in the fields to provide for Naomi and herself, Boaz can't help but notice this remarkable woman. Her determined spirit attracts him, piquing his curiosity and interest. Ruth's determination draws her into positive, thriving relationships.

What is so striking about a determined spirit? Why do stories of courage and tenacity inspire us? Why do we seek out and follow heroes who model wholehearted perseverance? How does another person's determination motivate us toward excellence?

---

*"By perseverance the snail reached the ark."*
***Charles Spurgeon***

---

The Bible clearly shows that perseverance is an outward expression of good character or integrity. Whether it's called courage, tenacity, resolve, determination, steadfastness or persistence—God calls us to model a commitment to him and his plans.

"Not only so, but we also rejoice in our sufferings, because we know that suffering produces perseverance; perseverance, character; and character, hope" (Romans 5:3-4).

"Create in me a pure heart, O God, and renew a steadfast spirit within me" (Psalm 51:10).

"Therefore, among God's churches we boast about your perseverance and faith in all the persecutions and trials you are enduring" (2 Thessalonians 1:4).

"To those who by persistence in doing good seek glory, honor and immortality, he will give eternal life" (Romans 2:7).

"But Christ is faithful as a son over God's house. And we are his house, if we hold on to our courage and the hope of which we boast" (Hebrews 3:6).

God continually models perseverance through his unwavering faithfulness. It's part of his nature. In spite of our doubt and disobedience, God persists in loving us with amazing, unconditional love. He pursues us with a fervent love. Aren't you drawn to the heart of your faithful Father? Doesn't his devotion pull you in again and again? Aren't you glad he is determined to love you—no matter how unlovable you are? How many times have you cried out in gratitude, thankful that he didn't give up on you? God's example of perseverance is the standard to which we must rise in all of our relationships.

---

*"Adversity causes some men to break;*
*others to break records."*
***William A. Ward***

---

**Obedient—Not Obstinate**

Determination is a hallmark of godly character. God doesn't want his people to be hopeless and discouraged—rather he expects them to be faithful and persistent. "For God did not give us a spirit of timidity, but a spirit of power, of love and of self-discipline" (2 Timothy 1:7). However, neither does God want his people to be stubborn. Let's be careful not to confuse stubbornness with determination. Whereas stubbornness is like a mule kicking and balking at every turn, determination is like a racehorse striving to cross the finish line victoriously. According to Scripture, a stubborn heart is disobedient (Romans 10:21), foolish (Ephesians 4:18) and destined to be destroyed (Proverbs 29:1).

In their first home Jody and Erik discovered a seemingly harmless plant in the yard. Being new to the area, they were unsure whether it was a weed or a flower, and so they let it go for a while to see if it would bloom. Bloom it did not—but grow it did indeed! As it turned out, the "harmless" plant was bindweed, a stubborn winding vine that quickly invades and strangles nearby plants. Its roots snake underground, making it nearly impossible to extricate. The bindweed was unaffected by a variety of weed killers. (Erik even thought it grew *better* when doused with weed killer!) After battling the bindweed for several years, Eric determined that the only way to completely get rid of the stubborn weed was to cover the area with landscaping plastic and decorative granite. Unfortunately that meant that in order to kill the weeds, the surrounding healthy grass had to die as well. Bindweed and stubbornness have much the same effect, strangling or overtaking all they touch. And just as much of the healthy grass had to die because of the bindweed, a stubborn heart destroys the healthy relationships that might have surrounded it.

To maintain healthy, thriving relationships, it's crucial that we have a solid understanding of the difference between a stubborn heart and a determined spirit. Consider the example of Moses and Pharaoh as they battled over the future of the Israelites. Moses was determined to carry out the Lord's commands. He persisted through hardships and frustrations, returning to Pharaoh repeatedly to demand the deliverance of the Israelites. His demands weren't selfish—they were ordained from God. He wasn't foolish—he was faithfully obeying God's direction. He wasn't heartless—it hurt Moses greatly to see his people suffering. He asked God, "O Lord, why have you brought trouble upon this people? Is this why you sent me?" (Exodus 5:23).

---

*"A man without determination*
*is but an untempered sword."*
***Chinese proverb***

---

By contrast, Pharaoh's refusals are an example of pure stubbornness. His actions are born out of selfish motives—he wants the Israelites as his slaves. His obstinate attitude is destructive—much of Egypt is destroyed through the steady rain of plagues. His stubbornness is hardhearted—the Egyptians must suffer the tremendous loss of their firstborn sons before Pharaoh (temporarily) changes his mind.

As we pursue godliness through perseverance, it's consequential that we understand the differences between determination and stubbornness. Our relationships will take two completely different paths, depending on the character we display. Consider these guidelines to help determine if your actions are persistent or stubborn:

☐ Am I honoring God through my actions?
☐ What is the final outcome I'm seeking?
☐ Will others have to suffer for my actions? If so, to what extent?
☐ Am I prayerfully seeking God in this matter—daily?
☐ Have I asked God if this is his will?
☐ Am I being destructive or productive?

Just as the bindweed appeared harmless at first, stubbornness can initially seem innocent. (We may even think it's a healthy sense of determination!) Pray and ask God to guard your heart and your actions from this destructive weed. Let your actions reflect *godly* persistence. Pursue a Christlike perseverance. Seek the heart of the Father to ensure that you are pressing on toward *his* goals.

**Naomi the Quitter**

Naomi had given up—and can you blame her? Her homeland had been plagued by famine, and so she had been forced to leave. Her husband died, followed by her two sons. She was advanced in years and had no grandchildren, no immediate family, no legacy. According to the standards of the time, Naomi seemingly had nothing. And so she gave up. "The LORD's hand has gone out against me!" she weeps (Ruth 1:13). "The Almighty has made my life very bitter . . . the LORD has brought me back empty . . . the LORD has afflicted me; the Almighty has brought misfortune upon me" (Ruth 1:20-21). In other words, "My life is rotten, and God did all of this to me!" Life is hopeless and bleak, so Naomi is giving up and going home. At least there she'll have a few friends and extended family members to mourn with her.

---

*"Few people are made of such strong fiber that they will make a costly outlay when surface work will pass as well in the market."*

***E. M. Bounds***

---

Have you ever been around someone like Naomi for a long time? Someone who is so soured on life that he or she has just given up? Their attitude is dismal, their words are depressing, and their countenance is gloomy. They make pessimistic Eeyore seem like a laugh-a-minute circus clown. How long do you stick around? How deep can that relationship go? When you come away from that person, how do you feel? Do you make efforts to spend increasing amounts of time together—or make excuses to avoid contact?

Relationships characterized by a sense of despair don't last long. Please don't misunderstand—we all have down times, or periods of sadness or loss. And just as God comforts us, we are called to comfort others and lead them through those times of distress. But a chronic attitude of depression will erode a relationship. A sense of passivity kills the joy of friendship or camaraderie. A pervading spirit of sorrow drowns the fires that kindle a relationship, just as water thrown on a campfire. For as we're drawn to someone who displays a sense of determination, we are equally repelled by hopelessness.

Jody's husband, Erik, had a stubborn wart on his toe. For

months doctors "burned" it with liquid nitrogen, cut away the skin and put special medications on it. Initially these painful procedures seemed to work, but the wart always came back in a few weeks. Doctors shook their heads, explaining that the *root* of the wart simply wouldn't die. Finally Erik was sent to a surgeon who used a laser to eliminate such persistent warts. How did the laser work? It seems that the laser, unlike the liquid nitrogen, cauterizes the blood vessels that flow to the wart. In other words, to kill the wart, they had to cut off the blood supply that was keeping it alive. Hopelessness kills relationships in the same way. It cuts off the supply of life-giving joy, leaving the person (and the relationship) to wither and die.

Naomi's attitude could have killed her relationship with Ruth. Her despondency could have cut off any joy or hope that Ruth wanted to pass along. Without Ruth's tenacity and commitment to Naomi, the two women would have been lost. Wallowing in her sorrow, Naomi would have wandered from God's ultimate plan for her life. Hopelessness destroys relationships because it destroys our vision. In Jeremiah 29:11 the prophet writes, " 'For I know the plans I have for you,' declares the LORD, 'plans to prosper you and not to harm you, plans to give you hope and a future.' " God's plans for us include hope. God has a vision for us. When we lose sight of that plan, we lose the vision. We lose hope.

**Satan's Power Tools**

Discouragement is an effective tool used by Satan to keep believers from accomplishing God's plans. "Hope deferred makes the heart sick" (Proverbs 13:12). Sick-hearted people don't have the passion or drive to live for God. Consider Job, whose own wife cried, "Are you still holding on to your integrity? Curse God and die!" (Job 2:9). In hopelessness Job's wife turned from God and encouraged her husband to do the same. Or reflect on the twelve Israelite spies who were sent to explore Canaan. Upon seeing the land that God had promised, they were disheartened and hopeless. "But the people who live there are powerful, and the cities are fortified and very large. . . . We can't attack those people; they are stronger than we are" (Numbers 13:28-31). Ten of the twelve spies spread such a discouraging and hopeless report that it angered God. He struck down those ten men, and they died (Numbers 14:37). God didn't want despair to choke the life and vision from his chosen people. He couldn't abide the thought of passivity overtaking the people to whom he had promised greatness.

Hopelessness is such an effective tool of Satan's because it robs us of our spiritual vitality—our passion for God. Without a thriving passion for our Lord we are useless to him. "I know your deeds, that you are neither cold nor hot. I wish you were either one or the other! So, because you are lukewarm—neither hot nor cold—I am about to spit you out of my mouth" (Revelation 3:15-16). In this passage the word *spit* literally means "vomit." In other words, God says, "Your passivity—your lack of passion—makes me sick!" Not only does chronic discouragement turn others away from us and sicken the heart of our Father, it turns others away from the heavenly Father. (And Satan would like nothing more than to turn people away from the King of Kings!) A passive and despondent heart cannot reflect the hope and faith that exemplify God.

If a sense of despair and hopelessness doesn't completely destroy a relationship, it *will* leave a skewed, one-sided relationship that will rapidly deteriorate.

Have you ever seen a miserably one-sided baseball game? I recall a time when Erik invited me to watch a church-league softball game in which he was playing. "The last time we played them, they only beat us by one run," Erik said. "If we beat them tonight, we'll be in first place!" Erik had his father-in-law pumped up, expecting to see a thrilling event. However, in the first inning the opposing team put twelve runs across home plate and went on to win 23 to 3. Ugh! As great as it is to be winning, after a while even the winning team gets tired of it. And the losers—they just want to finish and go home. How about the fans? Many will get up and leave, not wanting to see the painful and drawn-out conclusion. Those who stay will sigh and roll their eyes, frustration and impatience mounting. The sense of hopelessness is almost tangible. No one has a good time. The game is really over as soon as the losing team gives up hope.

God desires for us to "stay in the game." He doesn't want half-hearted players on his team. Similarly, a godly man or woman will long for relationships that are exemplified by perseverance. They will cultivate a sense of hope and persistence in others. They will encourage others toward healthy tenacity. They will view passivity in others as a relational obstacle—not an opportunity for domination.

**Hope Restored**

How odd, this attraction we have to persistence. When Jody's daughter Brianna was about eighteen months old, she was given a set of stacking cups that would "nest" when stacked in just the right order. Jody writes, "Erik and I loved to sit and watch Brianna work at those stacking cups, trying to get them to 'nest' just right. Her tenacity captured us, her determination surprised us, and her persistence delighted us. As parents we marveled at how focused this little mind was. It was a joy to see her commit to a task and resolve to finish it. When she accomplished her task, there was a tremendous sense of pride in all three of us!"

Determination is a powerful team-builder. Imagine what Boaz must have thought as he watched Ruth working. *Ahhh! I've heard of that woman—she's the one who came from so far away to care for her mother-in-law. And look at how hard she works in the fields. She's not just sitting around, waiting for someone to take pity on her. Wow, that's really something! I want to know more about this woman! I want her on my team!*

Ruth's determination attracted Boaz—not just romantically but in a deeper sense. Just as Jody and Erik marveled as they watched little Brianna work so hard at a difficult task, Boaz must have wondered as he watched Ruth take on incredible odds.

Hope creates a team spirit. Perhaps that's why Jesus continually gave hope to those he encountered. In order to build a strong team of believers, Jesus replaced despair with vibrant passion. He healed those who were terminally ill—without Jesus they would have given up hope. He raised those who had already died—without Jesus their loved ones assumed it was the end. He restored dignity to those who had lost it—without Jesus there was no reason to go on. By graciously pouring hope into the hopeless, Jesus drew people to the Father. *I want to be on Jesus' team!* they might have thought. *He believes in me—he never gave up on me! When I thought it was all over, Jesus showed me that it was just the beginning.* Jesus' team, made up of sinners, fishermen, tax collectors and beggars, had such tenacity and hope that they started a fire that's still burning today. Hope is a powerful magnet!

Jesus showed his disciples what it meant to persevere. He endured criticism, doubt, betrayal, faithlessness, pain, mockery and death. Through each trial he kept his eyes on the Heavenly Father, never losing sight of God's vision, never veering from God's plan. As a result, the disciples were a powerful team. From a handful of ragtag fishermen and tax collectors the church was born. These men and women were touched and motivated by Jesus' determination. Although they knew the road ahead would be difficult, Jesus had shown them that it was worth the effort.

---

*"There are important cases in which the difference*
*between half a heart and a whole heart*
*makes just the difference between signal defeat*
*and splendid victory."*
***A. K. Boyd***

---

What would such a "team spirit" do to your relationships? Imagine the possibilities if men and women were all in the game together rather than playing against each other! By displaying a sense of determination we foster unity. A spirit of perseverance conveys the message "I believe we can" instead of "Why even try—we're destined to fail." Just as Ruth's determination changed Naomi's life, our persistence can have life-changing effects on those we encounter.

**A Light in the Darkness**

The United States Holocaust Memorial Museum in Washington, D.C., is a somber and gripping place. Each of its four levels details a portion of the horror that left more than six million Jews dead between 1933 and 1945. It is a dark tour through history that you will never forget. Walking through the graphic and heart-wrenching exhibits, you can't help but feel overwhelmed by the sense of hopelessness and loss these people faced daily.

Yet in the midst of bleak tragedy there stands a bright light. On one floor is a large wall, listing the thousands of names of those who assisted the Jews during the Holocaust. These weren't necessarily strong or powerful people (although some of them *were* in prominent positions). They were shopkeepers, teachers, lawyers and business professionals. They were old and young, men and women, from numerous countries and backgrounds. Whether these individuals provided food, shelter, money, letters of transport or a new home, they all provided hope. Through their selfless efforts these people quietly restored hope to millions. Their bravery and commitment to humanity was a light in the darkness. They brought purpose when life seemed filled with despair.

Ruth brought a similar sense of purpose to Naomi's life. Perhaps her determination aroused Naomi's curiosity. "Life is terrible! What does that woman think there is to live for? Why does she insist on coming with me when there's clearly nothing in Judah for her? I wish she'd just leave me to wallow in my grief. But . . . hmmm, maybe she knows something I don't know. Maybe things *will* get better." Although we can only speculate, it's clear that Ruth's persistence gave Naomi a new outlook on life. After all, now she was no longer alone. She had someone younger and healthier to help provide for her needs. She had companionship. With Ruth's commitment came comfort and purpose. There just might be a reason to get up in the morning and get dressed!

Determination enriches a relationship, because it brings a sense of purpose. We are drawn to people who have direction in life, rather than those who seem to be stumbling around in the dark. Boaz could easily see that Ruth's life had purpose. Ruth was a woman who would get up each day with things to accomplish! The things Boaz heard and saw indicated that she was deliberate and determined. She had a goal in life, a purpose to every action. This sense of purpose is yet another characteristic that caught Boaz's attention and drew him toward Ruth.

In his first letter to the church of Corinth Paul writes, "Do you not know that in a race all the runners run, but only one gets the prize? Run in such a way as to get the prize. . . . I do not run like a man running aimlessly; I do not fight like a man beating the air" (1 Corinthians 9:24-26). Aimlessness gets us nowhere. God calls us to be purposeful and direct in our lives and in our relationship with him. Paul later wrote to the Philippian church, "Forgetting what is behind and straining toward what is ahead, I press on toward the goal to win the prize for which God has called me heavenward in Christ Jesus" (Philippians 3:13-14).

Do you sense the urgency—the excitement—in Paul's voice? His determination—his passion—calling these Christians to lives of purpose? Paul's passion was sharing the gospel. It motivated his every word and action. It drew people to him, attracting them, arousing their curiosity and turning their hearts toward God's. When our lives or our relationships have that same pure passion, we can't help but draw others in.

**The Pull of Persistence**

Let's return to the wall at the United States Holocaust Memorial Museum. The wall stands out because it's a beacon of hope in a place where tragedy abounds. The lives represented there symbolize determination and selflessness in the midst of despair and fear.

Although we may not live in the dire circumstances faced by the Jews of World War II, our world is pervaded by discouragement. Perhaps that is why God calls us to live lives of passion and perseverance. His plans for us are too great, his vision too amazing, for hopeless and despairing people. There may never be a memorial to you, but your determination may be the beacon that will save one person from a life of futility.

We are drawn to, motivated by and attracted to men and

women who model persistence in life. It's crucial that we realize that relationships characterized by a sense of hopelessness are unhealthy—destined to dissolve. By cultivating a spirit of determination in our own lives, we can begin to exhibit godly character and draw people to our heavenly Father.

I am convinced that Boaz was profoundly impressed by the unswerving resolve he observed in Ruth. He knew that deep within her there was a rich firmness of mind that would not let go of the godly convictions she had established. This determination gave her a beauty that awakened an admiration.

That's the challenge Ruth places before us. We are called to run the race with patient perseverance as we see the Lord Jesus at the goal line welcoming us home (Hebrews 12:1-2).

**What's Here for Us?**

1. Describe a time when you had to face what seemed like an insurmountable obstacle.

2. Would you describe yourself as "determined"? Why or why not?

3. What do you learn from Ruth that could strengthen your spirit of determination?

4. What issue are you presently facing that requires you to persevere?

5. Ruth nurtured perseverance in Naomi. Who needs your encouragement as he or she faces significant hurdles?

6. What things in life tend to "defeat" you? (Take a moment and pray, asking God to give you a spirit of determination when tackling those obstacles.)

# 9

# What's Mine Is Yours

PREACHER ROBINSON WAS FRUSTRATED BY THE LACK OF GIVING at Hollow Canyon Church. He preached, cajoled and even harassed his people to become generous givers. But the response was disappointing. Then one day as he was wrestling with the problem, he had a flash of inspiration.

The following Sunday he asked everyone to stand while the organist played the offertory hymn. Then he gave his listeners the following instructions: "Reach forward and take the wallet out of the pocket of the person in front of you. Now open it and give the amount you've always wanted to but felt you couldn't afford."

## The Root of Generosity

Like the folks at Hollow Canyon Church, most of us are not

known as generous givers. We convince ourselves that we barely have enough to meet our needs. So we clutch what we have more tightly. But when we watch Boaz, we see a man who didn't hold his resources with a tight fist but found joy in opening his hand to make a difference in Ruth and Naomi's lives. What prompts him to share freely? And why does he appear to do it joyfully?

We've already learned that Boaz's godliness was lived out in his daily activities. His life exhibited a loveliness that reminds us of Jesus Christ. So we shouldn't be surprised to discover that this scent of God has filtered into his attitude toward what his Lord had entrusted to him. Because he had come to a settled confidence in his Lord, Boaz was released from a self-centered focus and was freed up to turn his eyes toward the needs of others. We've noted earlier that he was a "blesser." His natural response was to give in a way that brought joy to those around him. A blesser always enriches other people's lives. They are looking for ways to share with those around them the riches they've received.

---

*"If you want to know what God thinks of money, you have only to look at some of the people he gives it to."*
***Anonymous***

---

Psychiatrist Karl Menninger observed that giving was a mark of mental health. He found that generous people are rarely mentally ill. Their focus is less likely to be inward. They do not have as great a need to hoard their resources. Generous individuals are less fearful that others will exploit them. Sharing their resources brings joy and fulfillment to their lives.

Allan demonstrates this attitude as he chats over the backyard fence with his neighbor about buying gifts for his wife, Sarah. "I think that I'm not the wisest guy when it comes to buying presents for Sarah," he says. "Probably my choices aren't the best. But bless her heart, she always receives them so graciously. What makes the difference is that she knows that I love her very much, and these bumbling efforts come from a loving heart." Allan isn't excusing his mistakes; he's thanking our Lord that Sarah can see the love that motivates his sometimes misguided actions.

**Two Kinds of Generosity**

We find it helpful to separate generosity into two categories: impersonal generosity and relational generosity. We define impersonal generosity as giving that costs us little or nothing. If a person has $1,000,000 in savings and gives $1,000, it really hasn't cost her that much. She still has $999,000 left for herself. A lot of what passes as generosity falls into this category.

Or imagine that we're walking down the street and a ragged, unkempt soul approaches us seeking a "donation." You rummage around in your pocket, extract a dollar bill and deposit it in his outstretched hand. He smiles, says "God bless you" and is on his way.

What did this act of generosity cost you? Little or nothing. The crumpled dollar bill will be quickly forgotten because you have lots more where that one came from. What's more, neither of us had to get involved in the homeless person's larger needs. We are free from active interest in his personal life. The fact that he suffers from intense loneliness and uses alcohol to numb the pain won't bother us because we didn't have to move to that level of relationship. We weren't about to make any commitment to help change his long-term circumstances. While we might have momentary feelings of pity, we have no intention of becoming emotionally involved. And we can quickly go on our way without interrupting our schedule or being inconvenienced.

---

*"It is so much easier to tell a person what to do with his problem than to stand with him in his pain."*
***David Augsburger***

---

Don't hear us say that impersonal giving is bad. You may give financially to support a missionary or contribute to your favorite college fund. These are commendable actions. But our point is they require no relationship with others other than slipping a check in the envelope, dropping some coins into the Salvation Army kettle and dropping the letter in the mail. They require financial commitment but little or no personal involvement, time commitment or emotional investment.

**Relational Giving: Opening My Life to You**

Some of the most profound and provocative verses in the Bible are found in 2 Corinthians 8:2-5, where the apostle Paul is bragging on the Macedonian Christians. He says:

> Out of the most severe trial, their overflowing joy and their extreme poverty welled up in rich generosity. For I testify that they gave as much as they were able, and even beyond their ability. Entirely on their own, they urgently pleaded with us for the privilege of sharing in this service to the saints. And they did not do as we expected, but they gave themselves first to the Lord and then to us in keeping with the Lord's will.

This amazing passage gives us some strong clues by which we can define relational generosity. Notice that the Macedonian's generosity

☐ came at personal cost
☐ was rooted in joy

- ☐ came without outside coercion
- ☐ went beyond normal expectations
- ☐ was rooted in devotion to our Lord
- ☐ cost them something of themselves

From this passage we can observe that relational generosity is a high-powered expression of love. Its high potency rests in its capacity to change another person's life in a profound way. And Paul gives us a clue as to what the source of this remarkable attitude is. He says, "We want you to know about *the grace that God* has given the Macedonian churches" (2 Corinthians 8:1, italics added). The purest form of relational generosity is rooted in the release of our Lord's grace in someone's life. His grace frees us to invest in others' lives.

Boaz was well acquainted with relational generosity. When Ruth entered his field on that fateful morning, she met a man who embodied this beautiful trait, and her life was forever changed. His words, "Stay here with my servant girls" (Ruth 2:8), express his desire to do more than make a onetime handout and go merrily on his way. He was inviting her to partake of his resources and come under his protective care.

Years ago I read a true account of this kind of generosity that was indelibly etched in my memory. The incident was told to Col. John W. Mansur during the Vietnam War.

An orphanage in a Vietnamese village had been struck by mortar fire. Missionaries and two children were killed, and several children were injured. One was an eight-year-old girl. When medical aid was sought, American military personnel responded. The navy doctor's examination revealed that a blood transfusion was imperative. Further tests revealed that some of the uninjured children's blood type matched the injured girl's.

Working through broken Vietnamese and sign language, the

medical personnel told the frightened children that unless some of the injured girl's blood could be replaced, she would die. Then they asked, "Would any of you be willing to give her your blood?"

---

*"Empathy is your pain in my heart."*
***Halford Luccock***

---

After a period of awkward silence a boy named Heng haltingly raised his hand. Quickly the young lad was laid on a mat beside the girl and a needle inserted into his vein. As the transfusion started, he suddenly covered his face and uttered a sob. The occasional sob turned into steady weeping. The medical team knew something was wrong but had no way to clearly communicate with the boy until a Vietnamese nurse arrived.

The nurse began a dialogue in her own language with the sobbing boy. As their conversation continued, his crying gradually ceased, and a sense of peace spread over his face. Then the nurse spoke to the American medical team and unraveled the boy's mysterious behavior.

"He thought he was dying. He misunderstood you. He thought you had asked him to give all his blood so the little girl could live."

A dumbfounded American nurse asked, "Why would he be willing to do that?"

When the Vietnamese nurse posed the question to the boy, he responded, "She's my friend."[1]

What distinguishes relational generosity from impersonal generosity is the willingness of the giver to give of himself. Relational generosity costs the giver a price that others are often not willing to pay. It may cost personal freedom, public scorn, involvement in another's problems, and so on, but the giver forgoes these "privileges" to seek a higher good for someone else.

**What Did Boaz Give Ruth?**

The relational giver does not overlook the obvious. He sees those things people need and endeavors to make their situation more tolerable. Boaz recognized that Ruth had been working diligently through the morning hours. Gleaning was hot, dusty work, leaving a person tired and thirsty. So Boaz said, "Whenever you are thirsty, go and get a drink from the water jars" (Ruth 2:9).

But in this simple action Boaz gives Ruth something greater. *He invites her to enjoy unearned privileges.* One Bible scholar notes that "she must not go to any other field than his; she must not be treated like ordinary gleaners, but remain *there,* where he had spoken to her, 'by the maidens,' so that, as the reapers went forward, and maidens after them to bind the sheaves, she might be the first to glean; *she must share the privileges of his household;* and he must take care that she should be unmolested."[2]

But notice that Boaz's generous actions gave Ruth some less obvious but even more crucial benefits. For one thing, *he gave her hope.* It's certain that when she left the field that day and walked the dusty path back home, a new sense of hope beat in her breast. Coming to the field that morning she could only hope that she could glean enough grain for her and Naomi to have a meal. Suddenly through Boaz's generosity there will be food on their table for the entire harvest season. Her heart must have overflowed with joy as she returned home that evening.

Second, Boaz gave Ruth *a renewed sense of dignity.* Rather than treating her as an outcast—like someone to be endured—he opened his heart to her and made clear that he would view her as someone worthy of his respect. He also made crystal clear to the men in his fields that they were to treat her with dignity. No insulting remarks. No crude jokes at her expense. She was not to be a pawn for their appetites. He would have none of that.

---

*"My riches consist not in the extent of my possessions but in the fewness of my wants."*
***J. Brotherton***

---

Most of us have opportunities every day to extend Boaz's relational generosity to someone and "make their day." One student in nurses training learned this from her professor. The last question on a pop quiz was "What is the first name of the woman who cleans the school?" The student's initial response was, "This has to be some kind of joke!" She had seen the tall, fiftyish woman at work but felt no obligation to know her name.

Following the exam a student asked if that question would count on the grade. "Absolutely," the professor exclaimed. "In your careers you will meet many people. All are significant. They deserve your attention and care, even if all you do is smile and say hello."

The individual who related this incident said, "I've never forgotten that lesson. I also learned her name was Dorothy."[3]

Third, Boaz gave Ruth *a sense of security.* Finally that nagging sense of insecurity that had clung to her was gone. Someone had said that he would look out for her interests. He would protect her. Her welfare would be his concern. All of us have observed many individuals who live in a constant state of vulnerability because no one wants to get involved.

Fourth, *Boaz affirmed Ruth.* He expressed his admiration of her. Listen to his words: "I've been told all about what you have done for your mother-in-law since the death of your husband—how you left your father and mother and your homeland and came to live with a people you did not know before. May the LORD repay you for what you have done" (Ruth 2:11-12).

What a life-changing gift for someone who may have felt like the lowest person in Bethlehem's social register. The newest foreigner from a pagan country isn't likely to be invited to the annual ball. The story of Cinderella makes a great children's tale, but when we grow up, we decide that's not the way for us big folk.

Boaz reaffirms his admiration of her months later near the close of the harvest season. He says, "All my fellow townsmen know that you are a woman of noble character" (Ruth 3:11). His own actions communicate that he too believes this and holds her in high esteem.

Relational generosity doesn't lock people into social castes. It doesn't condemn individuals to past failures. It doesn't judge us according to ethnic prejudices. The man or woman who practices relational generosity finds joy in lifting others up, in affirming their strengths and in communicating worth.

Last, *Boaz gives Ruth his time.* This may seem like an odd example of relational generosity, but it is one of our most valuable possessions and one of the most practical gifts we can give. We live in a busy, hectic world. Sometimes the greatest gift we give others is the gift of time. I was reminded of this recently when I went to visit a retired colleague who is now living in a care center. As I visited with my esteemed friend, I realized that to spend time with him was one of the most precious gifts I could give. I came away from that encounter determining to make that a priority in the coming months.

### Jesus' Affirmation

Our natural tendency is to identify giving with giving *things.* But the greater giving is when we give those intangible actions that *touch the person's heart* and communicate love and valuing.

Jesus told a parable that affirmed our heavenly Father's commitment to transform our lives through relational generosity.

In Luke 15 he related the account of a young man eager to taste the "real world." To accomplish this the young man brazenly sought his inheritance while his father was living. The father granted him his request, and in a flash the son joined up with a partying crowd in a far city. Soon his resources were depleted. Then his partying friends departed, and he was left in a destitute condition. He exhausted every means to stay alive, and in final desperation he decided to return to Dad and plead for an opportunity to become a servant. (It's obvious he knew that he didn't deserve any family privileges. He'd insulted his father by his request and his actions.)

Jesus then described the ragged young man's return home and the father's reaction. The father's relational generosity is mind boggling. He generously gave the son those elements that would restore him. First, he gave his son *unconditional love*. Dad ran to this undeserving, pig-scented son, threw his arms around him and kissed him fervently. Second, he instructed his servant to bring *the best robe* and put it on his son. The point is not the monetary value of the robe but the message that is sent by *covering his shame* with something beautiful and valuable.

Third, the son was given a ring that would *establish his identity* as a full-fledged member of the family. In a tangible way he knew that his dad didn't want a servant, he wanted a son. Fourth, the son was given sandals to cover his feet. That might seem like a small thing to us in today's world, but in Jesus' day servants went barefooted; family members wore sandals. It was a testimony to the community that this *boy is my son, not my slave.* And finally, the dad said, "Let's throw a party and celebrate. I've got my son back, and I'm thrilled to death."

What do all these generous actions accomplish? Do they leave the son feeling financially wealthy? No. Rather they leave him feeling relationally wealthy. He knows that he is loved; he knows that he is accepted; he knows that he is forgiven. And these are the things that change a person's life and fill one with indescribable joy.

---

*"Few rich people own their own property.*
*The property owns them."*
***Robert Ingersoll***

---

**The Power of Relational Giving**

When we give as Boaz gave, as the father of the prodigal gave and as Jesus Christ himself gave—giving himself for the church that he might make her holy, pure and radiant (Ephesians 5:26-27)—we will leave an impact on others just as these three did. A person can be financially impoverished but give in a more significant way than the wealthiest man in the world.

Why is this so?

☐ Relational giving senses an individual's real needs and joyfully shares resources that can make a difference in that person's life. In that sense it is a powerful expression of our Lord's passionate love.

☐ Relational generosity changes another's life. By this we become ministers of our Lord's grace, which stimulates the soul of the receiver and communicates life and hope. Like Ruth and the prodigal son, this kind of generosity jump starts many people's lives, giving them inner encouragement and motivation, as well as practical help.

☐ Relational giving nurtures health in others. Through Boaz's generosity, we are told, Ruth "was filled and satisfied" (Ruth 2:14), and she had something leftover to share with Naomi. We see in this a picture of the person who receives health and then has resources to share with others contributing to their restoration. Ruth and Naomi became restored, fulfilled, productive individuals through the generosity of one man.

☐ Relational giving stimulates the spirit of gratitude in others. In 1918 on the battlefield in France, Robert MacCormack saved his commanding officer's life. Every year for over twenty-five years Major Harry Parkin wrote a letter of thanks to MacCormack. In his twenty-fifth letter he wrote, "I want to thank you for the twenty-five years of life which ordinarily I would not have had were it not for you. I am grateful to you."[4]

☐ Relational generosity fills the giver with the joy that comes from investing in another's life. Many of us have been touched by the wise words of Jim Elliott, who gave his life to share the gospel with the Auca Indians. He said, "He is no fool who gives that which he cannot keep to gain that which he cannot lose." Those are the words of a Boaz.

**Does it Matter?**

What difference does it make if we cultivate this lovely quality in our lives? Is it really that important? We think the answer is a resounding *yes*!

I've provided you with three significant examples of relational generosity—giving of ourselves and our resources in a way that changes people's lives. What difference did it make in Ruth's life, in the prodigal son's life and in our lives—those whom Jesus Christ gave himself to redeem?

Boaz's actions brought a complete transformation in Ruth's destiny. Apart from him she would have remained an alien resident widow struggling in poverty. But Boaz's generosity led to

Ruth's becoming the great-grandmother of David, perhaps the greatest king in Israel's history. And she was a vital link in Jesus Christ's earthly lineage.

And what about the prodigal son? Though this was a parable, it implies that the son had a second chance to become a productive person. The father's generosity allowed the full restoration of the relationship. It opened the door for the son's confession of his ungodly actions. He had the joy of knowing beyond a doubt that he had been forgiven.

And you and me? No one has given more sacrificially than our Savior, Jesus Christ, that we might become the children of the God of heaven and earth, whom we get to call Father. We get to spend eternity in his presence because his beloved Son was so relationally generous.

When I was in the sixth grade, my family lived on a farm in a remote section of southwestern New York state. I went to a two-room school in the little burg of Cameron. One day in the hurry to catch the bus I forgot my lunch. At noontime only one person offered to share his lunch with me. An orphan boy named John Dibble had hard crusted biscuits in his lunch pail. He shared what little he had with me.

I can't remember another person who attended that school with me. Only John Dibble. I've never forgotten how he had the least of anyone there, but he was willing to share with me. I've long forgotten what the biscuits tasted like, but I've never forgotten John Dibble's kind generosity.

### What's Here for Us?

1. I described my memories of John Dibble's generosity. Imagine that you were going to nominate someone for the "Most Generous Person" award (someone who has been generous to you). Name and describe that person.

2. This chapter introduces the idea of "relational generosity." Give an example of a time when you were relationally generous.

3. What is the biggest cost for a person to be relationally generous?

4. What other Bible characters model relational generosity to us?

5. What two people that you relate to need your generosity? How would it change their circumstances? How might it change them?

6. How would you compare your attitude toward generosity with that of Boaz? What have you learned from him?

7. Reread the passage in 2 Corinthians 8 concerning the Macedonian Christians. Then evaluate your own attitude and practice toward investing in others' lives.

8. Can you think of a time when someone's generosity gave you renewed hope?

9. Who comes to your mind as someone who serves humbly? What could you do that would communicate appreciation and affirmation?

# 10

# Humility

## *Love in Service*

HOUSTON ROCKETS COACH RUDY TOMJANOVICH WAS CURIOUS, so he asked each of his twelve players a question. He wanted to know who they believed should have his hands on the ball with ten seconds left and the score tied. What he was essentially asking was, Who do you trust to make the play? Who is the best player on our team? Who can get the job done? The results? A twelve-way tie.[1] Each player thought that he would be the best man for the job. So much for teamwork!

Although it's likely that the NBA is the wrong place to look for examples of humility, the search for a humble heart is often just as difficult in our own lives. Unlike submissiveness (which we wrote about in chapter four), today's society *does* value humility. Look at the fairy tales we tell our children from the time they're toddlers: Snow White, the beautiful but humble princess who goes about her work with a smile and a song; Cinderella, the sweet servant who dutifully attends to her proud stepsisters' every whim; even the story of the shoemaker and the elves, in which poor elves selflessly assist a struggling shoemaker. In every case the main character's humility is commended and eventually rewarded.

We're undoubtedly drawn to people who display the tender attitude of a servant, but we're fearful of taking that role ourselves. Men *and* women are afraid that a humble attitude will somehow demean them. Humility is a virtue we extol yet one we too often hesitate to cultivate in our own relationships. We are touched when others display a spirit of modesty, but we (often subconsciously) jockey for position as "top dog." Why? Perhaps we're looking through our eyes rather than through God's eyes.

The Bible repeatedly gives examples of the power and influence of a humble heart. It's clear that God not only values modesty and meekness, but he expects us to display these attributes in all we do and say. Think of it this way: *God* is attracted to humility. Meekness and lowliness make God smile. If these characteristics are attractive to God, and we are made in God's image, how much more are they appealing to us and those whose lives we touch?

Ruth is characterized by her humility. Her servant's heart pervades her every action and brings an incredible peace to all of her relationships. She took the role of a servant—caring for Naomi, putting her own needs aside, working hard in the fields, associating herself with servants and accepting the help of others. Ruth's example will help us more clearly understand what it looks like to be a servant today and the incredible influence that such an attitude can have on our relationships.

**Down to Earth**

First, it's important that we share the same definition of humility. Most of us tend to associate humility with embarrassment or humiliation. Words like *meek, lowly, poor* or *plain* come to mind, along with uncomfortable memories of red-faced blunders we've made. But the Bible shows us God's view of a humble heart—the attitude of a servant. Jesus says, "Come to me, all you who are weary and burdened, and I will give you rest. Take my yoke upon you and learn from me, for I am gentle and humble in heart, and you will find rest for your souls" (Matthew 11:28-29). Think of humility as "love taking the position to serve another." As we explore the allure of a humble heart, bear in mind that we mean a loving, servant's heart. It is the desire to serve and to put another's needs ahead of our own.

---

*"The beauty of humility is that we become empowered to respect others."*
***Gary Thomas***

---

The root of the word *humble* comes from the Latin word *humus*, meaning "earth."[2] It's very possible that we get the phrase "down to earth" from this origin. Down to earth is an excellent way to describe Ruth. She was unassuming, putting aside her own cultural need for a husband to serve and care for her mother-in-law, Naomi. Naomi says to Ruth and Orpah, "May the LORD grant that each of you will find rest in the home of another husband" (Ruth 1:9). In Ruth's time a husband provided more than companionship and family. He provided a woman with status, a name, financial support and a heritage through children. Ruth's sacrifice for Naomi is enormous. What's even more incredible is that she expects nothing in return. Ruth doesn't proclaim, "I'll take care of you if you take care of me." She never bargains, "I'll be your traveling companion if you give me a place to stay." Her sacrifice comes purely from a loving, servant's heart.

Women today aren't strangers to this kind of servanthood. Most mothers display such humility without a thought when it comes to their children. When a child cries in the night, a mother will give up hours of sleep without hesitation. When there's only one slice of pizza left, she offers it to her children first. And when a child and a mother both need new shoes, who do you think will get them first? "Motherly humility" doesn't include conditions or regulations. It's simply based on selfless love.

Transfer the example of a mother's love to your other relationships. How does that humility look when

☐ you're asked to make changes on a big project at work?

☐ your spouse needs a break from the kids for a few hours . . . and so do you?

☐ a neighbor is moving and asks for help?

☐ the toddler Sunday school class doesn't have a teacher?

☐ an elderly relative is lonely?

☐ you've made a mistake that will affect others?

Humility today looks just like it did in Ruth's time. She lovingly put the needs of others before her own. She served without hesitation. She willingly took a lowly position, doing menial work to provide for those she loved. She put pride aside and tenderly cared for those around her—without any guarantee of reward or reciprocation. In fact, the absence of pride has a profound effect on Ruth's relationships. It can make an unimaginable difference in our relationships as well.

**The Poisonous Power of Pride**

A relationship characterized by prideful attitudes is one that is destined for trouble. Think back to our fairy tale examples: Snow White's wicked stepmother is destroyed in the end; Cinderella's selfish stepsisters gain nothing (and lose everything) from their haughtiness; in another tale the emperor's pride is eventually his downfall when he is caught naked in public. If Ruth had acted with pride, she and Naomi may have starved and would likely have been alienated by those around them. Pride could very well have left Ruth a poor widow for the rest of her life.

---

*"I believe that the first test of a truly great man is humility."*
***John Ruskin***

---

The subtleties and consequences of pride may not be so easy to identify in our own lives. We may not notice it, nor do we recognize the damaging effect pride is having upon our hearts and our relationships. Subtle pride is an effective tool that Satan uses to drive us further from God and from achieving godliness in our lives. The Bible repeatedly states God's view of pride:

☐ "The LORD's curse is on the house of the wicked, but he blesses the home of the righteous. He mocks proud mockers but gives grace to the humble" (Proverbs 3:33-34).

☐ "The LORD detests all the proud of heart. Be sure of this: They will not go unpunished" (Proverbs 16:5).

☐ "Though the LORD is on high, he looks upon the lowly, but the proud he knows from afar" (Psalm 138:6).

☐ "Do not be proud . . . do not be conceited" (Romans 12:16).

**Funhouse Mirrors and Broken Hearts**

Through the Bible God also provides us with examples of people who could attribute their troubles (or complete demise) to pride. Samson, King Saul, David, Balaam, Lot and Nabal are just a few who let arrogance or selfish intentions ruin the opportunities God had placed before them. Satan even tried to tempt Jesus with self-seeking words. Satan reminded Jesus of the awesome power Jesus possessed. The great deceiver dangled power and majesty like a carrot for Jesus to chase. But Jesus knew that he would not accomplish his mission on earth through using his power for his own needs. Jesus accepted humility for the greater purpose of our salvation.

---

*"The first principle of servant leadership is: Servant leaders humble themselves and wait for God to exalt them."*
***C. Gene Wilkes***

---

To further examine the destructive power of pride, let's take a closer look at Nabal, a powerful and conceited man introduced in 1 Samuel 25. Months after David's armies had graciously protected Nabal's shepherds and flocks against thieves, David sent men to Nabal, kindly asking him for simple compensation for their services. But Nabal's conceit distorted his view of himself and of David. He responds arrogantly, refusing to provide anything—and even insults David in the process. David's response is swift and violent. He immediately tells his men, "Put on your swords!" (1 Samuel 25:13). Through foolishness and pride Nabal dies (although not at the hand of David but at the hand of the Lord).

It's easy to find the fault in Nabal, but pride does the same thing to us today. Arrogance blows up our ego, hiding the clear picture of who we really are. On the heels of our success Satan paints a distorted image that convinces us that we are mightier or more worthy than we truly are. Even if our vision is skewed a little, Satan's goal is accomplished. Pride often shapes our perception like a funhouse mirror. Have you ever looked into a series of funhouse mirrors? For a while it's amusing to see your figure change in ways you never thought possible. (Haven't you always wanted legs that were ten feet long?) But isn't it a relief when you finally look in a regular mirror? Isn't it good to know

"That's what I *really* look like. That's *really* me"? Even if the image isn't perfect, there is comfort in the truth.

---

*"Show me thy humble heart, and not thy knee."*
***William Shakespeare***

---

Pride not only damages *our* hearts, it damages the hearts of those around us. Nabal's conceit angered David, causing him to raise up four hundred men against Nabal's household. People react in the same way today.

April 20, 1999, two young men in Littleton, Colorado, opened fire on their classmates at Columbine High School. They came armed with semi-automatic weapons, pistols and numerous homemade bombs designed to maximize death and destruction. When the dust settled, fifteen people were dead. As families, friends and investigators tried to answer the burning question "Why?" one fact kept appearing. The boys saw themselves as outcasts, alienated by the teens around them. They'd been told they didn't measure up, that they didn't fit in. Running up against a wall of pride, they turned to hate.

Think back to the beginning of this chapter, to the example of the Houston Rockets. After such a poll, what must each player have thought about his teammates? *They don't trust me. What a self-serving bunch of yahoos! Don't they think I'm good enough?* How could these feelings affect teamwork? Doubt, frustration and dissention creep in, alienating us from one another. Pride is unquestionably destructive.

---

*"Humility is the hallmark of the man whom God can use, although it is not in the world's curriculum."*
***J. Oswald Sanders***

---

Jesus told the disciples, "What comes out of a man is what makes him 'unclean.' For from within, out of men's hearts come evil thoughts, sexual immorality, theft, murder, adultery, greed, malice, deceit, lewdness, envy, slander, arrogance and folly. All these evils come from inside and make a man 'unclean' " (Mark 7:20-23). Can you see why Jesus puts arrogance on the same playing field with murder? Pride destroys our relationships from the inside out. It is powerful. It is subtle. It is poison to our hearts and minds.

With God's help we can maintain an unclouded image, so pride doesn't have to gain a foothold in our hearts and minds.

☐ Following any success, pray. Thank God for the victory.

☐ Surround yourself with wise people who can gently "hold up a mirror" to remind you of your true reflection.

☐ Think before you speak. (Remember, Nabal's quick reaction was an expression of the arrogance in his heart.)

☐ Remember the power and subtlety of pride. It usually isn't overt. Read aloud Mark 7:20-23 as a reminder of the seriousness of a haughty heart. (You might also check out Romans 1:29-31.)

☐ Make praise your passion. First and foremost, praise God. Turn your attention away from your own desires and focus on him. Praise others, celebrating their victories and affirming their accomplishments. The joy you find in selflessness is a sure way to purge pride from your heart.

**The Healing Hand of Humility**

Whereas pride destroys, humility nurtures life and growth. In the face of poisonous pride, a humble heart offers healing. Ruth's humility nurtured every relationship she was involved in. Naomi responded with friendship, Boaz responded with a marriage proposal, and those around Ruth spoke well of her (Ruth 2:11-12). Her modesty attracted others in indescribable ways.

As I mentioned before, God is attracted to humility too. Read through the Bible and you can't miss God's desire for us to love with a servant's heart.

"When pride comes, then comes disgrace, but with humility comes wisdom" (Proverbs 11:2).

"This is the one I esteem: he who is humble and contrite in spirit, and trembles at my word" (Isaiah 66:2).

"The greatest among you will be your servant. For whoever exalts himself will be humbled, and whoever humbles himself will be exalted" (Matthew 23:11-12).

"All of you, clothe yourselves with humility toward one another" (1 Peter 5:5).

---

*"Pride changed angels into devils;*
*humility makes men into angels."*
***Augustine***

---

God's ultimate example of humility was displayed through Jesus. God could have come as a prince, or at least a man from a wealthy and important family. But God appeared to us a helpless child, born in a lowly stable, of average lineage. He took an unassuming trade, owned few possessions and spent most of his time with common (even undesirable) people. Jesus didn't simply live this way because he wanted to show his humility. He was a living example of how you and I are to live. Jesus' humility—which ultimately ended in victory—brought healing, peace and redemption to the world. Humility can have the same effects on our relationships today.

**Two-Way Service**

An interesting observation about Ruth: the more she served, the more others were inclined to serve her. As Ruth cared for Naomi day after day, Naomi began to offer help and service to

Ruth. Similarly, as Ruth worked in Boaz's fields, Boaz provided more food, increased safety and (finally) his own name. That's because *humility nurtures mutual serving of one another*. A humble heart is so attractive that we're encouraged to model the behavior ourselves!

---

*"It is hard for a 'superior' person to be used of the Lord."*
***Richard Halverson***

---

However, it's important to note that this is only the case when we model *sincere* humility. Our agenda needs to be one of service and love, not our own edification.

At the time of this writing Jody and her husband are expecting the birth of their second child. They've been gently preparing their two year old, Brianna, for a new baby sister or brother, explaining what it might be like with a baby in the house. What has been amazing has been Brianna's response. Jody writes, "We've tried to be honest, explaining that sometimes the baby will be noisy and will want to play with Bree's toys. Rather than complain or sulk about the news, Brianna has reacted with joy. She is excited to serve the baby. She talks about pushing the baby in the stroller or helping the baby choose a toy. She even wants to tickle the baby when he or she cries!"

---

*"Someone asked one of the ancient Fathers how he might obtain true humility, and he answered: 'By keeping your eyes off other people's faults, and fixing them on your own.' "*
***Alphonse Rodriguez***

---

Brianna has been on the receiving end of Jody and Erik's love and service. Even at her young age she knows the warmth of a hug, the delight of a walk in the sun and the joy of being tickled. And she wants to pass those things on to her sibling. Jody and Erik didn't show affection and servanthood to Brianna just so she would show it to others. It came from a pure heart of love. In the same way our acts of humility must be done purely from love rather than from the anticipation of returned service.

**A Heart Magnet**

Another effect of a servant's heart is that it attracts others and draws them to us. Just as Boaz was drawn to Ruth, we are drawn to a heart that is willing to serve. Think of someone you like to spend time with—someone you truly enjoy being around. What do you enjoy about that person? What keeps you coming back for more? It's likely that the person demonstrates, in one form or another, a servant's heart. Why are we drawn to humility?

- ☐ We know we'll be heard.
- ☐ We know we'll be served.
- ☐ We know we'll be helped.
- ☐ We know that our needs will matter.
- ☐ We know that there will be peace.
- ☐ We know that God's heart will be present.

Jody's supervisor was recently interviewing applicants for a job opening. The top candidate wasn't the one with the most experience or even the most knowledge. The supervisor thoughtfully said, "There's a humility—a teachable spirit—about her that's really appealing." To this man a servant's heart was a crucial characteristic. It set the candidate apart from others. It made the difference and made his decision easy.

---

*"Oh beware! Do not seek to be something! Let me be nothing, and Christ be all in all."*
***John Wesley***

---

Because humility draws others closer, there is more time for the relationship to grow. Therefore, humility is a key to developing deep, mature relationships. Consider the example of Jesus and his relationship with his disciples. God knew that it was vital that Jesus teach and impart wisdom in the short time he spent on earth. In order for God's love to be understood and his message communicated, it was critical that people spend time with Jesus. Jesus' humility drew people in and kept them coming back for more. If Jesus had been arrogant or pompous, it's likely that the disciples would have chosen to spend their time elsewhere. But these men gave up everything to follow Jesus. His teachings touched them, but his humility and love kept them at his side.

Consider the impact you can have for Christ, through the use of this "heart magnet" we call humility. Not only do you have the opportunity to display the Father's heart, but you'll draw others closer, enabling relationships to deepen and allowing prolonged exposure to God's love. A person who displays Christlike humility is a powerful tool for our heavenly Father.

**The End Result**

The Bible clearly and repeatedly speaks of the ultimate result of a humble servant's heart—victory and redemption. God poured out blessings on Abram, even though Abram had allowed Lot to choose the "better" land (Genesis 13:8-17). Rahab's life was preserved—as well as the life of her family—when she served the Israelite spies (Joshua 2:1—6:23). Esther risked her life, saved her people and initiated the holy day of Purim (Esther 1—10). The woman who anointed Jesus' feet was praised and exalted for her humility (Mark 4:3-9).

And let's return for a moment to the story of Nabal, for we would miss the best part if we left Abigail out. Abigail, Nabal's wife, learned of her husband's selfish response. In her wisdom she immediately gathered generous quantities of food, drink and supplies. Rather than simply send a servant, she brought the gifts to David and his men. "When Abigail saw David, she quickly got off her donkey and bowed down before David with her face to the ground. She fell at his feet and said: 'My lord, let the blame be on me alone. Please let your servant speak to you; hear what your servant has to say' " (1 Samuel 25:23-24). Abigail goes on to humble herself and praise David, exalting his triumphs and the Lord's hand in David's victory. The result? "David said to Abigail, 'Praise be to the LORD, the God of Israel who has sent you today to meet me. May you be blessed for your good judgment' " (1 Samuel 25:32-33). Not only was Abigail's home and family spared from David's wrath, but after Nabal's death, David returned and married her! Abigail's humble heart brought peace, redemption, blessing and renewed relationship. Do you believe that servanthood is just as powerful today?

---

*"Humility is to make a right estimate of one's self."*
***Charles Spurgeon***

---

Humility catches the eye and captures the heart. It is a powerful, healing balm for our relationships. Just as God sent Jesus to humbly serve, he desires to send us into the world with the same attitude.

How can you reach out with humility today? What effect will your actions have? What stumbling blocks keep you from serving others? Pray and ask God to remove those barriers that only hinder deeper relationships. Seek his guidance as you serve others. And look for the incredible growth in your relationships and in your own heart.

**What's Here for Us?**

1. Study what the Bible says about our Lord's humility.

2. Where does pride show itself in your life?

3. Identify someone in your life who displays humility. Think of three specific ways that they willingly take the role of a servant. Now think about the other relationships that person has. What do others say about him or her?

4. What difference could a humble heart make in your relationships? (Think of family relationships, friendships and even business relations.)

5. Personally, what draws you to a humble heart?

6. How can you strive to act with humility today?

# 11

# The Incredible Power of a Redemptive Lifestyle

MANY YEARS AGO IN NUREMBERG, GERMANY, TWO YOUNG lads, Albrecht Dürer and Franz Kingstein, trained and toiled to become artists. Both showed promise and each dreamed of becoming famous.

As time passed, it became obvious that Albrecht's skills were those of a genius. But Franz was not gifted and would never be more than an art lover. Each had undertaken a rendering of the passion of Christ. When Franz viewed Albrecht's lovely etching, he lifted his hands in an act of despair.

"Albrecht, it's hopeless. I can never become an artist," he cried. "You will be famous; I never will be."

Albrecht responded quickly, "Hold your hands just as they are. Don't move them. You, too, shall be famous." Then the gifted artist grabbed his brush and painted the hands that have become famous as "The Praying Hands."[1]

Not all of us have the same talents, gifts and opportunities. But we all have something that can strengthen, bless or enrich others' lives. We can use our resources to give them a productive future.

Can you recall someone who has had a significant influence on your life? Someone who left his or her mark on you? One of my former seminary students told me of a college teacher who saw creative potential in him. She affirmed it, nurtured it in the classroom and watched him become a creative, fruitful person. Now many years later the student is leaving his own mark on others.

### Old Testament Redemption

Our Lord placed an important principle in the Old Testament as a part of his loving care for his people. It's referred to as the kinsman redeemer concept, which we touched upon earlier in chapter three. It was a way to lovingly protect and provide for his people when they were in distress. He didn't leave them without someone to rescue them. The idea is described in Leviticus and Deuteronomy with three situations identified in which a kinsman redeemer would be needed.

*Redeeming another's lost land.* In Leviticus 25:23 we read, "The land must not be sold permanently, because the land is mine and you are but aliens and my tenants. Throughout the country that you hold as a possession, you must provide for the redemption of the land. If one of your countrymen becomes poor and sells some of his property, his nearest relative is to come and redeem what his countryman has sold." A close relative would have the privilege of buying back land for his kinsman.

Our Lord cares about his people. He says to them, "I don't want you to lose the land, and if you become so poor that you have to sell the land to exist, there is somebody in your family, a kinsman, that should go back and say, 'I want to buy that land back for you. Here's the money.' "

*Redeeming another from slavery.* Then God outlines a second way redemption was to occur for an Israelite. In Leviticus 25:47 he describes a situation in which a Jew might become so poor that he would sell himself into slavery to an alien living in the land. In that circumstance we read, "One of his relatives may redeem him; an uncle or a cousin or any blood relative in his clan may redeem him." In other words, a prosperous foreigner settles in Israel. He's got a lot of money, and in order to stay alive the Israelite sells himself into slavery to this person. But since our compassionate God doesn't want any of his children enslaved, he made a way to secure their freedom.

*Redeeming another's lost legacy.* Deuteronomy 25 describes a third way redemption could occur—another loving provision for his people. In verse 5 we read, "If brothers are living together and one of them dies without a son, his widow must not marry outside the family. Her husband's brother shall take her and marry her and fulfill the duty of a brother-in-law to her. The first son she bears shall carry on the name of the dead brother so that his name will not be blotted out from Israel."

Can you feel our Lord's tenderness in this provision? If your brother dies, you marry his wife and the first child born will carry your brother's name so his memory won't be blotted out. That seems unusual to our way of thinking, but it was God's loving concern for his people. He cared that a brother's legacy would continue.

These three provisions remind us of how loving our heavenly Father's thoughts are toward you and me. Jesus said, "Look at the birds of the air; they do not sow or reap or store away in barns, and yet your heavenly Father feeds them. Are you not much more valuable than they?" (Matthew 6:26). Unfortunately many of us have never grasped how personal our Father's commitment is to our care.

**Modern-Day Redemption**

Now that we have a capsule idea of how redemption functioned among the Israelites, we can ask ourselves some questions. What does the root concept tell us about our Lord? What underlying truth does it communicate to us today? What would it look like in action?

First, redemption speaks of releasing or freeing someone from bondage or oppression. Somewhere there is always someone being oppressed, chained by some form of bondage. Someone seeks relief from a backbreaking burden. Some are enslaved to drug or alcohol addiction. Others are held hostage through intimidation or threats of violence. Then there are people who feel helpless because severe poverty leaves them trapped in hopelessness.

I met a woman in Rochester, New York, who had felt the power of a redeemer. I was sitting at her breakfast table talking with her and her husband. This is what I heard:

> The person sitting beside me was used of God to transform my life. I had always felt as though I was a nobody, a person with no value, a person that had nothing to offer others. But my husband's constant affirmation began to penetrate my heart. He helped me see how precious I was to our Lord. He consistently identified my strengths. He opened my eyes to see who I really am. I'm a different person today because I married him.

Second, redemption is release from fear or anxiety. I may be anxious because I don't know how I'm going to pay my bills. Or I may lie awake at night fearful that someone may break into my house and cause physical harm to my family and me. How I wish I could have a few moments of peace. If only there was a deliverer.

Third, we need to be delivered from the bondage of sin. All of us were born in sin. We've felt the judgment of sin. But the Bible tells us that Jesus Christ is the great Redeemer, freeing me from sin's penalty and slavery, and filling me with the joy of forgiveness. I don't have the curse of sin over me. I'm redeemed.

**Boaz: A Kinsman-Redeemer in Action**

Boaz is *the* Old Testament example of a redeemer in action. And his actions are pivotal to understanding the message of the book of Ruth. When we opened the pages of this book, we discovered two women trapped by their life circumstances. Ruth and Naomi are in dire need. Their poverty is great. Their future looks bleak. Then a man enters their lives and unties the shackles that bind them. Through Boaz they experience the joyous feeling of release. "We've been set free. Hallelujah! We have hope!"

What we see in Boaz is a picture of what it means to be a redemptive person—to set someone free. There are at least three things Boaz models to us about being a redemptive person.

**Redeemers Make It a Way of Life**

First, *Boaz models redemption as a way of life—a lifestyle.* Doing it one time is great, but our Lord calls us to a redemptive lifestyle. When we follow in Boaz's steps, we can clearly see his commitment to make a difference in other people's lives. When he is introduced to us in chapter 2 of the book of Ruth, he immediately displays a redemptive attitude. He enters the field where the reapers are hard at work and calls out, "May the LORD be with you." Then in verse 5 he asks, "Whose young woman is that?" He's looking out and observing and watching and seeing where people are around him. According to the text he's a lot more interested in his people than in his crops.

Obviously he was an excellent businessman and farmer. But his heart is for people, and he excels as a redeemer. He isn't poring over his books to see how he can get the biggest crops and how he can outwit somebody else. Rather he's using his resources—using everything he has within him—to minister to people. *Helping people is Boaz's passion.*

I know a businessman named Jim. In the early years of his profession he was concerned about his business, making a profit and so on. But then there came a turning point in his life when he began to view his business as *a context for ministry* to touch people's lives. Everything changed. He began to take an interest in his employees in a new way. He'd enter the front door in the morning and instead of going directly to his office he'd stop and chat with all twelve to fifteen employees. Jim would say, "How are you doing this morning?" "How is your family?" All of a sudden they began to realize, *He cares about me. He has an interest in me. I'm not just an employee; I'm a person!*

Jim took an interest in the way employees worked together. He even brought in a specialist to help him and to help other workers work out personality differences and learn communication skills. He had shifted from merely being a sharp businessman to being a Christian man who took an interest in the people around him. He was becoming a redemptive person.

Boaz challenges us to say, "My heart is with people. I see someone over there and I say, 'Tell me about this person. I'm interested in this person.' She happens to be a social outcast. Could you tell me more about her? Maybe she is a person I could help in some tangible way."

The incident in Ruth 2:14-16 demonstrates this. A hungry

woman stands before Boaz. She doesn't have food. He says, "Come over here. Have some bread and dip it in the wine vinegar." So she sits down beside the reapers and Boaz serves her roasted grain.

Isn't that a touching thought? *He serves her.* Here is what in our culture would be considered a business owner and a street person. He asks someone else, "Who's that person?" and when he finds out he says, "Come over here and let me serve you some food." That's redemptive. That's his fundamental attitude. That's who he is.

You'll notice that when Boaz is around people, he is blessing them. That is the heart of the redeemer. Always wanting to impart God's gift to them—to bring joy or cheer into their life. It's a lifestyle. It's not an isolated act that we did for somebody today—like giving a person a dollar to get a cup of coffee. No. He enters into a relationship and asks himself, *How can I make a difference in somebody's life?*

**Redeemers Enrich Others' Lives**

There's a second thing Boaz models for us. Notice *Boaz's commitment to enrich other people's lives.* Boaz's blessing arises from a genuine desire to give others a better future. He doesn't give Ruth a handout and then send her on her way with a "Have a nice day." A Boaz wants to make a long-term difference in another's life. A Boaz wants what's best for others. He wants their lives to be more than it would be if he weren't around.

**Making a Difference in Others' Lives**

Let's ask the question, "In what specific ways do Boaz's actions change Ruth and Naomi's lives?" Or "How were they different because he came into their lives?"

For one thing, we discover that Naomi is changed from a bitter woman to a joyful woman. Remember one of the things we said in our definition of being a redeemer: a redeemer leads a person out of anxiety and fear and bitterness, into joy and freedom and peace. Naomi is a transformed person because the redeemer comes into her life. When she left Israel, went to Moab and returned, she'd changed from pleasant to bitter (Ruth 1:20). From the time she returned until her grandson is born, she has changed from bitter to joyful (Ruth 4:14-16).

Their lives are different because Boaz redeems them from a life of poverty to a life of abundance. He redeems them from a life of insecurity to a life of security. He redeems them from an uncertain future to a promising future. They will no longer have to wake up in the morning and wonder where the rent money will come from or how they will buy food.

Boaz's actions also give these two women new identities. Nobody will be likely to treat Ruth as a second-class citizen any longer. If they do, they'll have to deal with Boaz! Ruth has instant status in the community. Someone might call her "Ruth the Moabitess," but he'd better not treat her like a Moabitess. She'll be treated like Boaz's wife. That's a huge transformation!

Boaz also gives Ruth and Naomi a larger sense of family. When they arrived in Bethlehem, they were bound as mother-in-law and daughter-in-law. In a sense Boaz gives them back what they had lost.

We think that Naomi senses the potential blessing that Boaz could bring to their lives. When Ruth comes home to Naomi that first day, Naomi knows something significant is happening. She seems to be saying, "You've got an awful lot of grain here! What's going on? Something happened!" Then at the threshing floor Boaz lavishes Ruth with his generosity. He says, "Wait a minute. Don't go back empty-handed. Hold out your skirt," and he fills it up. Ruth goes home and what does Naomi think? *Boy. Something is happening. We've got a redeemer in our life who is mighty generous.*

**Redeemers Glorify Their God**

Boaz models something else for us—something very beautiful. He demonstrates to us *that giving our life away for others produces great glory to our God.* In Ruth 4:14 the women of the village say to Naomi, "Praise be to the LORD, who this day has not left you without a kinsman-redeemer." Do you see the effect of Boaz's actions on others? They are glorifying God. It's as though they are saying, "God has done a remarkable thing! We never thought Naomi would have a chance. Truly, God is great!"

God is being glorified in the midst of Boaz's godly actions. The neighbors were glorifying God, but do you realize that it went far beyond this? *For generations people have given glory to God for what Boaz accomplished in his God's name.* When we arrive at the end of the book of Ruth, we know the rest of the story. We know that this son born of Ruth and Boaz was the forefather of Israel's great king David and ultimately in the lineage of Jesus Christ, the ultimate Redeemer. The infant Obed is God's channel through whom the Savior, Jesus Christ, will come.

Remember, Ruth and Boaz are people like you and me, who want to honor the God they love. Ruth is a woman who comes from a pagan heritage and into the land in poverty with no standing, comes in with her mother-in-law, who is equally destitute. Boaz says, "I will redeem you. I will buy you back from the curses upon your life." Out of that relationship a little child is born—Obed. When you read the lineage of Jesus Christ, you'll find Ruth. This nobody without any hope is now in the greatest family tree one could ever dream of having. Is God going to get any glory? You'd better believe it.

Do you believe this remarkable truth? *We never know how far our life will extend.* Heaven will hold breathtaking surprises for many who think what they do is unimportant. Amid the hallelujahs and hugs many will be honored for simple, yet life-changing acts of redemption. And the greatest thrill will be when our Lord Jesus looks into seemingly insignificant individuals' eyes and says, "Well done. I appreciate the redeeming love you've shown to __________ and __________ and __________."

Have you ever pondered the fact that the only ones that we know for sure go to heaven are people? It's a romantic thought that our beloved dogs and cats would go there, but we only know for sure that redeemed men and women will arrive at those pearly gates. So the greatest investments ever made are investments in people, because only people go to heaven. And our experience has been that we cannot begin to grasp the way our loving redemptive actions will affect people for eternity.

**For Example**

About fifty-three years ago in the back corner of a little Baptist church, a young Sunday school teacher named Mr. Rice told a backward, insecure twelve-year-old boy from a pagan heritage about Jesus Christ. He related how God had sent his Son to die on the cross for that lad's sins. He said that if the boy would trust Jesus Christ as his Savior, he could have a home in heaven with Jesus. That was the greatest news the boy had ever heard. Following his teacher's leading, he prayed a simple prayer of faith and trusted in what Jesus Christ did on his behalf.

The Sunday school teacher encouraged, loved and taught the boy for about a year without seeing a lot of change. No great transformation occurred, but the Sunday school teacher would come by the boy's house, and they'd go to church together. About a year later the boy moved away to his grandparent's farm, and that was the last that Sunday school teacher saw of him. Just a backward kid who had bowed his head and said, "I receive Jesus Christ into my heart." That Sunday school teacher, in fifty-two years, as far as I know, has no knowledge of what happened to the shy, backward, unpromising boy. He might not even remember him! But fifty-two years ago that man, who was an instrument of God, was a redeemer who pointed that lad to the great Redeemer.

That twelve-year-old boy was Norm Wakefield. Do you think Mr. Rice has any idea of the glory he's brought to God? This young boy had found hope in Jesus Christ and our heavenly Father, in His faithfulness, kept him and fed him and nurtured him, and grew him, and let him have the joy of sharing the Word of God with you. All he did was to lovingly tell a twelve-year-old boy about Jesus and befriend him for a year. But think of what God has done in his great mercy because someone was the redeemer to someone else.

Do you see the point I'm making? It's unlikely that Mr. Rice could grasp the significance of what our Lord was doing in my life or the fruit that would come from his redemptive ministry to my life. But Boaz reminds us that the Lord "is able to do immeasurably more than all we ask or imagine, according to his power that is a work within us" (Ephesians 3:20).

**Modern-Day Redeemers**

Do redeemers like Boaz live today? I can answer that with an emphatic yes. And I'd like to give you two more examples.

Angie is a friend who lives in southern California. I've known her for a number of years. Life has been hard for her. I've watched her life deteriorate into a pattern of consistent fear and anxiety. Much of it was rooted in unresolved issues from her past that continued to keep her in a personal hell.

One day Angie called and in a despairing voice said, "I'm suicidal and have to get admitted to a psychiatric hospital." Hospital and counseling fees skyrocketed to thousands of dollars. She was released, but she was still dealing with significant issues. She started going to a church family that was profoundly caring. They developed a pattern of loving care in which compassionate and gifted individuals would consistently gather around this hurting woman and, while laying hands on her, pray for her week after week. Praying for her, loving her and befriending her, they were committed to being instruments of our Lord's healing in Angie's life.

And redemption occurred. I have seen the transformation take place. Angie has been redeemed from the curse that plagued her life. When I saw her a couple of weeks ago, she exhibited a spirit of peace and joy that was beautiful to watch. She talked about her future. She was happy in the Lord. Somebody had been a redeemer for her. They prayed for her in faith. They surrounded her, loved her and protected her. Now Angie is being a redeemer for others.

I've seen redemption occur in our own family. A few years ago one of my brothers telephoned and wanted to know if I would do a thirty-fifth wedding renewal for his wife and him. Their marriage had occurred under difficult circumstances. They didn't have a personal relationship with Jesus Christ and were caught in a destructive lifestyle. My sister-in-law had carried shame from those early years.

Thirty-five years later we had a wedding renewal. Now both of them had a vital relationship with Christ. They had six children and a host of grandchildren. All lined the front of the church for this special event. One of the sons had been asked to express thoughts on behalf of the adult children to their parents. So a burly son, with tears streaming down his cheeks, stood and told his mother and dad how much he thanked God for them. Between sobs he gave this tribute to his parents, who had come to know and honor their Lord. It was a thrilling experience of affirming their faithfulness.

Little did we know that our Lord was using this event to redeem my sister-in-law from her shame. A curse was lifted off of her shoulders that none of us had known about. In a later conversation she said, "That did something for me. The affirmation of God's blessing upon our marriage now. For years I've had this shadow of failure and shadow of shame." As a result of the redemptive affirmation of children and friends, she had become a more joyful woman. Something destructive had been lifted off of her shoulders and replaced with a blessing. That's redemption.

We have the privilege of standing in the name of Jesus and blessing other people and ministering to them, and buying back .heir lives in some way in the name of Jesus Christ. To us that's one of the greatest opportunities we have, and every one of us can be a part of it.

What we're saying is that redemptive acts change people's lives. Their lives become enriched. Where there was poverty, there is wealth. Where there was fear, there is peace. Redemption, within the body of Christ, issues in fruitfulness. Do you remember what Naomi said to Ruth and Orpah as they were getting ready to leave Moab? "I can't give you any children. If I could get married and have a son, would you wait for him to become an adult and marry him?" What is she saying? I have nothing I can give you. No fruitfulness.

But when we come to the end of Ruth, in chapter 4, verse 13, here are two women who came into the land barren. "So Boaz took Ruth"—he had literally redeemed her—"and she became his wife. Then he went to her, and the Lord enabled her to conceive, and she gave birth to a son." Isn't that interesting?

And we've seen that the village women affirmed the Lord's blessing on Naomi when they said, "May he become famous throughout Israel. He will renew your life and sustain you in your old age."

So it isn't just Ruth now who is fruitful; Naomi, too, is fruitful. She would have never had a grandson. She would have gone to her grave with no heritage. Today the redeemer, Boaz, has redeemed these two women. We can see Naomi prancing around the village, "Look what I got!" You'd better believe every woman in Bethlehem knew the redeemer was there, and she had fruit for her life. Ruth is fruitful, Naomi is fruitful, and the community took a second look at these two ladies because now they are fruitful.

**Have You Caught the Vision?**

Have you caught the vision of being a redemptive person? Is that your daily lifestyle? After all, that's what we've been talking about. Is there a friend that you're investing in? Are you a redemptive spouse—or parent? (A lady wrote me a letter and said, "I've come to the conclusion that I want to be a redemptive mother to my two children.") What do you have that others can be blessed by?

With great conviction we're challenging you to see the potential of your life as it's invested in others in acts of loving kindness that will touch their hearts. We're convinced that the redemptive lifestyle is a joyous reality because it bears fruit in other people's lives and it will bear fruit for all eternity. It may be reflected in being a friend to someone who needs to know that someone loves him or her. It may be using some God-given talent to help another grow or achieve a goal. It may be taking a boy fishing who has no parent who will do it. It may be helping someone find a vital relationship with the ultimate Redeemer, Jesus Christ.

Opportunities are unlimited. Think of that person who is enslaved with an addictive habit. What could you offer that would make a difference? Who is the person near you who would profit from your mentoring?

It's possible you're saying, "I'm a nobody!" Do you think Ruth might have felt like she was a nobody? Now think of how God used her to bring joy and delight to Naomi and Boaz.

Moses bowed before the Lord on Mt. Sinai. God was calling him to be a redeemer for the Israelites who were enslaved in Egypt. Moses used every excuse in the book to say that he was unequipped for the task. But our Lord even used the shepherd's staff in his hand to perform miracles. Let your God surprise you with what he will do with what you offer him to bless others. God is filled with surprises. Let him surprise you.

**What's Here for Us?**

1. In this chapter we've been talking about a redemptive person. Describe a person who has redeemed you in some way.

2. What did Boaz lose when he redeemed Ruth? What did he gain?

3. Why do you think the near kinsman decided not to redeem Ruth (see Ruth 4)?

4. What would it look like if Christian men and women lived more redemptively toward each other?

5. In what way does this chapter challenge you? Who could you act more redemptively toward?

## Notes

**Chapter 3: A Man of Grace**

[1]Robert J. Morgan, "June 28," in *On This Day* (Nashville: Thomas Nelson, 1997).

[2]"March 18," in ibid.

[3]W. G. Heslop, *Rubies from Ruth* (Grand Rapids, Mich.: Zondervan, 1944), p 80

**Chapter 5: Godliness**

[1]*Arizona Republic,* June 16, 1991, p. 5C.

**Chapter 6: Not the Brightest Bulb**

[1]Max Lucado, *In the Eye of the Storm* (Dallas: Word, 1991), pp. 115-22.

[2]Lawrence O. Richards, *Zondervan's Expository Dictionary of Bible Words* (Grand Rapids, Mich.: Zondervan), p. 286.

**Chapter 7: Gentlemen Versus Gentle Men**

[1]*Webster's New Collegiate Dictionary,* ed. Frederick C. Mish (Springfield, Mass.: Merriam-Webster, 1985), p. 475.

[2]Herbert Victor Prochnow, *The Public Speaker's Treasure Chest* (New York: Harper & Row), p. 344.

[3]Tryon Edwards, *The New Dictionary of Thoughts* (New York: Standard, 1960), p. 232.

[4]Charles L. Wallis, ed., *A Treasury of Sermon Illustrations* (New York: Abingdon-Cokesbury, 1950), p. 57.

[5]David Aikman, "Meekness That Matters," *Moody Monthly,* February 1993, p. 31.

**Chapter 8: A Firm Resolve—A Steadfast Heart**

[1]Michael Hart, *The 100: A Ranking of the Most Influential Persons in History* (New York: Citadel, 1992), p. 188.

**Chapter 9: What's Mine Is Yours**

[1]*Missileer,* February 13, 1987, p. 4 (a newspaper for Patrick Air Force Base, Florida).

[2]Alfred Edershein, *Old Testament Bible History* (Grand Rapids, Mich.: Eerd-

mans, 1984), p. 184, emphasis added.
[3]Taken from the Internet.
[4]Robert G. Lee, *Sourcebook of 500 Illustrations* (Grand Rapids, Mich.: Zondervan, 1964), p. 147.

**Chapter 10: Humility**
[1]"Fast Break," *The Denver Post*, April 25, 1999, p. 21C.
[2]*Webster's New Collegiate Dictionary*, p. 586.

**Chapter 11: The Incredible Power of a Redemptive Lifestyle**
[1]*Treasury of Sermon Illustrations*, p. 160.